NINJA BANDICOOTS AND TURBO-CHARGED WOMBATS

NINJA BANDICOOTS AND TURBO-CHARGED WOMBATS

STORIES FROM BEHIND THE SCENES AT THE ZOO

HAZEL FLYNN

PiccoloNERO

Published by Piccolo Nero,
an imprint of Schwartz Books Pty Ltd
Level 1, 221 Drummond Street
Carlton VIC 3053, Australia
enquiries@blackincbooks.com
www.nerobooks.com

9781760641672 (paperback)
9781743821138 (ebook)

A catalogue record for this book is available from the National Library of Australia

Cover and text design by Akiko Chan
Illustrations by Miranda Sofroniou

Photos courtesy of Zoos Victoria: Tim Bawden (Leadbeater's Possum); Jo Howell (Mountain Pygmy-possum, wombat, Tasmanian Devils); Will Watt (Eastern Barred Bandicoot); Rick Hammond (platypus, Baw Baw Frog, Southern Corroboree Frog, Wedge-tailed Eagle, Orange-bellied Parrot, Guthega Skink, tree-kangaroo); Megan Croucher (koala, koala joey).

Printed in Australia by McPherson's Printing Group

For my sister, Aileen, lifelong carer
for creatures great and small

CONTENTS

Introduction

Have you visited your local zoo or animal sanctuary lately? If you have, you might have heard a zookeeper tell an amazing tale – perhaps the one about the orang-utan who figured out how to unscrew the bolts on his enclosure, or the young female elephant that enjoys the digeridoo but hates bagpipes, or the gorillas who love having music by Beethoven played to them. But zookeepers do a lot more than entertain visitors.

Keepers develop close, respectful relationships with the animals they care for. They also train them so that the animals don't have to be poked or prodded against their will. These days, lions, tigers and bears willingly cosy up to the side of their enclosure so their keepers can check their paws for sores, feed them medicine or even give them an injection. Likewise, emus, which are usually difficult creatures to weigh, now jump onto their scales, while wombats walk willingly into their boxes for transport.

Zoo staff also work way beyond the zoo grounds. Out in the bush, zoo scientists are rescuing Endangered species like the Baw Baw frog, figuring out how to breed them in the zoo and then returning them to the wild.

In this book, we take you behind the scenes at Melbourne Zoo and Healesville Sanctuary, a zoo for Australian native animals located on the outskirts of Melbourne. Turn the page to meet dedicated zookeepers and zoologists who work there, and find out how they are safeguarding the future of the animals they love.

1

Forest Fairies and Frozen Fur

Leadbeater's Possums and Mountain Pygmy-possums

Eric Wilkinson had always loved the bush and learning about nature. At the age of eight he read a story about Leadbeater's Possums in a magazine called *Wild Life*. Though none had been seen for almost 40 years, the man who wrote the story wasn't prepared to give up on them. Charles Brazenor worked at a museum in Melbourne and when he went through specimen drawers no one had opened for years, he found a taxidermied Leadbeater's Possum that had been donated long ago and completely forgotten about.

Charles put a massive effort into trying to track down the person who had found the possum originally, hoping they might help him find more that were still alive. He didn't have much more to go on than the surname Wilson and the location – a town in the Dandenong Ranges – but he travelled out there and knocked on the door of every person named Wilson in the whole district. He didn't find the person he was looking for, but he did hear from someone who had known Wilson and could tell him the mountain where the possum had been found.

At last, a promising lead! Charles spent many days and nights slogging up and down the densely forested mountain, hunting for any sign that the little possums still existed. He found nothing. But there were other mountains to explore in Victoria's Central Highlands, where the elusive possum had once been so plentiful.

In order to enlist others to his cause, Charles wrote the article that young Eric would later read, calling on "all good nature lovers" to send him an urgent message if they thought they'd ever sighted a Leadbeater's Possum. But no messages came. Ten years later, the Leadbeater's Possum was officially declared extinct.

Charles Brazenor went on to become the director of the museum. Eric grew up and studied at university to become a geologist specialising in fossils. After graduating he went to work as an assistant at Charles's museum. When they weren't working, Eric and his friends liked to go out into the bush and observe the

LEADBEATER'S POSSUMS: FAST FACTS

They are:

Mammals: The mothers make milk for their babies.

Marsupials: The tiny babies go straight into their mother's pouch after birth and stay there until they are big enough to move around on their own.

Nocturnal: They are active at night.

They were originally known as: Bass River Possums.

Their scientific name is: *Gymnobelideus leadbeateri.* The first word comes from the Greek for 'naked' (*gymno*) and 'dart' or 'arrow' (*belideus*). They got this name because they resemble Sugar Gliders (*Belideus*) in the way they move from tree to tree, but they lack a gliding membrane (making them 'naked'). The second word recognises Museum of Victoria taxidermist John Leadbeater, who preserved the first specimens.

Their babies are called: joeys.

Their average lifespan is: five years in the wild, up to 13 in captivity.

The biggest threats they face are: loss of habitat due to logging and bushfires.

Their conservation status is: Critically Endangered.

birds and animals, keeping note of what they had seen and taking photographs when they could.

On one of these night trips in 1961, not long after he got the museum job, 22-year-old Eric was sure he'd seen a Leadbeater's Possum. One moment it was there, and then it was gone. But the instant he caught sight of it, a feeling like electricity shot through him and the hairs stood up on the back of his neck. He was certain of what he had seen, but could it really be so? Was it possible? Had he really just spotted an 'extinct' animal?

With his mind still racing, Eric got back in the car for the drive home to Melbourne. Five minutes down the road, a nightjar – a brownish, medium-sized bird that's active at night – flew across the car's path and landed on a branch. Eric got out to observe it, and there, on the same tree, was a Leadbeater's Possum! This one didn't move. He got a good long look at it through his binoculars.

At first glance a Leadbeater's Possum could be mistaken for a Sugar Glider, except for the tail. The Leadbeater's tail is shaped like a baseball bat, narrow where it joins onto their body, then flaring wider

MOUNTAIN PYGMY-POSSUMS: FAST FACTS

They are:

Mammals: The mothers make milk for their babies.

Marsupials: The tiny babies go straight into their mother's pouch after birth and stay there until they are big enough to move around on their own.

Nocturnal: They are active at night.

Their scientific name is: *Burramys parvus*. They were given this name, which means 'small rock mouse', by Scottish-born amateur palaeontologist Robert Broom in the 1890s. Broom never saw the possums. He only had pieces of Ice Age fossils to go on; the animals themselves were believed to be long extinct.

Their babies are called: joeys.

Their average lifespan is: one to two years (for males) and one to three (for females) in the wild; eight to 10 (for both sexes) in captivity.

The biggest threats they face are: loss of habitat due to the building and expansion of ski resorts and roads; climate change; and feral predators (cats and dogs).

Their conservation status is: Critically Endangered.

along its length. That's exactly what Eric could see through the magnified lenses. There was absolutely no doubt about it. These elfin creatures had eluded humans for half a century and now young Eric had stumbled on two in one night! No wonder that even in his seventies, his voice still cracked with emotion when he described it.

Eric's discovery should have marked a happy new beginning for Leadbeater's Possums – they hadn't been extinct after all, they had just stayed out of sight all those years. The Victorian government even made the possum the official state animal. But the truth is these special little animals are now dangerously close to *really* disappearing forever.

There are two separate surviving populations of Leadbeater's Possums: one in a lowland swamp forest near Yellingbo in the Yarra Valley, and one in the Central Highlands near Marysville. They face different types of threats.

Farmland has expanded around the Yellingbo habitat, leaving just a ribbon of forest. This naturally damp swamp area has been damaged by the farms' water needs. In its natural state, the swamp would regularly flood and drain, but now emptied of water for farming, the trees have begun to die off. And that means the possums that lived in and fed from those trees have also died off.

More than 20 possum families have been lost. From a once thriving population there are now fewer than 40 possums left. These small numbers mean it is very difficult to successfully produce offspring that will grow up and have babies of their own. So Zoos Victoria has taken in some of the Yellingbo animals to care for them and try to develop a captive breeding program, with the aim of releasing young ones back into the wild. As the world's foremost expert on these possums, Dr Dan Harley, says, "Taking them into captivity is not a step to be taken lightly, and reflects how dire things have become in the wild."

This program began in 2012 but so far no babies have been produced. Possum keeper Paula Watson has been working on it from the beginning. She says all the conditions are right for the possums to be mating, but it's just not happening: "We're a little bit suspicious it's the males that are not doing the job, which could be diet-related. So we're working on the diet side of things

CRYPTIC ANIMALS

Both Leadbeater's Possums and Mountain Pygmy-possums are known as 'cryptic' animals. But that doesn't mean they're good at solving tricky crosswords. In biology, describing an animal as 'cryptic' can have a couple of different meanings. For scientists who specialise in analysing DNA, 'cryptic' refers to animals that *appear* to be identical but turn out to be two different species. Examples include "the African elephant". Studying its genes proved it is actually two distinct species (now referred to as the African elephant and the African bush elephant). But for zookeepers such as Paula Watson, 'cryptic' means animals whose appearance or behaviour (or both) makes them extraordinarily hard to spot in the wild. Spiders that look like ants and cuttlefish that change colour to blend in with the ocean floor are cryptic because of their appearance. For the possums, it's more about behaviour: being nocturnal and either extremely fast, quiet and hard to spot (Leadbeater's); or spending most of their time hidden from human sight in boulder fields (Mountain Pygmy-possums).

now. Trying to navigate the ins and outs of a breeding program is very tricky. You need a lot of patience."

Paula has always loved being around animals. At a very early age she decided she wanted to help them in whatever way she could. She says, "I don't know where it came from, but I always liked being outside and playing with bugs and watching baby birds. I used to keep snails as pets, and when I was about 10 I made an insect hospital from a little cardboard box divided into different wards with cotton-wool beds and tissue sheets, and I had a whole set of rules and regulations for it that I wrote in my diary."

After finishing school, Paula studied veterinary nursing, then worked as a vet nurse for many years. She originally went to Healesville Sanctuary to do vet nursing but moved over into zookeeping. "I've always had a soft spot for native animals," she says. "I worked with kangaroos and koalas and platypuses and dingoes and some bird species and I enjoyed them all, but I wanted to be involved in the conservation side of things. I've worked with Mountain Pygmy-possums since 2008 and Leadbeater's Possums since 2012. I really love my job. I love working with animals every day and feeling like I'm making a difference for threatened species."

There are 2000 Leadbeater's Possums in the Central Highlands, which sounds like a big population compared to Yellingbo, but is actually a worryingly small number for an entire species, especially one under huge pressure from logging.

Back in 2009, the numbers were more than twice this. Then came the catastrophic Black Saturday bushfires. While some kangaroos and other animals managed to flee the ferocious fire front, these tiny possums weren't able to. The fires destroyed nearly half the population and the trees they lived in. Protecting the survivors and their remaining habitat became even more important.

The problem is that the trees these possums need to survive are the same ones the timber industry cuts down to create wood and paper products. Standing in the middle of these forests, you can tilt your head as far back as it will go and still not see the tops of the trees. The mountain ash that grows here is the world's tallest flowering plant. It can grow up to 100 metres tall over its 400-year life. Leadbeater's Possums live in family groups inside hollows in these old-growth trees and each hollow takes about 150 to 200 years to develop.

But the possums need other kinds of trees too, particularly wattles (or acacias), which they rely on for food. They carry the bark of eucalypts or paperbark back to their hollows with their tails and use it to make elaborate cosy nests that look like woven baskets. They also need what's called an understorey – the bushes and low trees that grow on the forest floor. Because they don't have gliding membranes as Sugar Gliders do, these possums run between trees rather than leaping from one to another; without an understorey to hide in they are easy pickings for predators.

Timber harvesters aren't interested in the wattle trees or the understorey, but it all gets smashed in the process of chopping down and removing the taller trees, destroying the habitat the possums need to survive. We need timber to build houses and for lots of other purposes, but many environmental experts believe that timber should not come from these old-growth forests, which are so rich in irreplaceable wildlife. They argue we should be developing plantation forests, grown especially to be harvested.

Fortunately the government of Victoria now agrees but it took a while to happen. As part of the efforts to stop logging of old-growth forests, hundreds of ordinary people who care about the survival of the possums volunteered their time to go into the forests to look for the 'forest fairies'. They recorded the sightings on infra-red and thermal video and reported the GPS coordinates. More than 3000 hectares of possum habitat has been identified and protected with help from these citizen scientists.

*

The Leadbeater's Possums weren't the only possum to be rediscovered in the 1960s. Just six years after Eric's discovery, a visitor to the University Ski Lodge at Mt Higginbotham saw a little creature darting behind the stove – but it didn't look quite like a mouse. His friends helped him capture it and sent it off for identification. By matching it to Ice Age fossils, it was found to be a Mountain Pygmy-possum, believed to be extinct. However, not one other of its kind could be found for quite a while. Because of that, the 1967 *Guinness Book of Records* named the Mountain

Pygmy-possum the rarest animal on Earth, although scientists later carried out surveys and found several populations, all in high alpine areas.

Mountain Pygmy-possums are tiny. About the size of a mouse (which makes them around one-third the size of Leadbeater's Possums), they can easily fit into the palm of your hand when they're curled up asleep. They're Australia's only hibernating marsupial and are alpine specialists. They spend up to seven months curled up tightly, deep between the mountain snow. But snowy mountain areas are also popular with people, of course: the areas where the possums live – on Mt Buller, Mt Higginbotham and Mt Kosciuszko – have been developed into some of the country's busiest and most popular ski fields.

In Mt Buller, for instance, some of the most popular downhill runs are directly above the Mountain Pygmy-possums' main breeding area. People skiing down Federation Slope are passing above possums hibernating amid the boulders deep beneath the snow.

As part of the National Recovery Plan put in place to help the species survive, ski field operators now work to protect the possums and their habitat. But a lot of the resorts and roads were built before people realised the effects they would have on the possums. Boulders are an obstacle to builders, so when roads and ski resorts were constructed in those areas it was common to use dynamite to smash the big rocks to smithereens. But Mountain Pygmy-possums need the boulders to survive.

They live in what are known as boulder fields: sprawling rivers of rock created by glaciers thousands of years ago. 'Fields' makes them sounds flat, as if a single layer of boulders was scattered across the surface of the mountain. But just like a river of water, these are three-dimensional and in some places very deep. There is plenty of room between the rocks and boulders for the possums to move about without having to come up to the surface, where they could be attacked by predators.

In winter, when the temperature drops and heavy snow falls, the possums make their way deep down among the boulders. Here, they survive the three months of extreme cold and lack of food by hibernating. There's a lot more to it than just going to sleep.

They take a small store of seeds with them for snacks, then curl themselves into a furball to conserve heat.

Paula Watson explains: "They spiral their tail up and press it like a flat disc on their tummy or hold it in their paws. They've got biggish ears for a little marsupial, and they fold them right down on their heads. They pull their arms and legs in tight and they tuck their heads down as far as they will go – females put the tip of their nose into their pouch."

Then their body temperature drops and drops. When they're not hibernating, their temperature is around 37°C, like ours. But when they enter what's known as torpor, it drops to a level that would be deadly for humans, just 2°C – that's colder than the air inside your fridge! Up above, the air temperature can get as low as –20°C, but the snow acts as insulation, keeping the temperature where the possums are a couple of degrees above zero, which suits them just fine. From time to time, during hibernation, they rouse to nibble on some seeds. Early in winter they do this every couple of days, but as the snow gets thicker above them, they only stir every 20 days or so.

When spring arrives, bringing warmer weather, the snow begins to melt. The possums' internal body clocks tell them it's time for hibernation to end. To get back up to their 'normal operating temperature' they shiver so hard you'd be worried for them if you saw it happening. By contracting their muscles like this they produce heat and warm themselves back up.

In captivity, if the keepers think the males are hibernating a bit too long, they will give them a hand to wake up – literally. The almost frozen little possums are brought out of their chilled hibernation area and held in someone's cupped hands for half an hour. There's never any shortage of volunteers for that job. "The more you handle them and stimulate them, the more they'll start breathing, and you can feel their body go from cold back to normal temperature," says Paula. "They go through a phase called semi-torpor where they're not quite with it. They're kind of fuzzy-headed and squinty. It's really cute."

The males, which live separately from the females in the wild, emerge first and when they do, they are famished. They need to eat, and they need to eat NOW! Mountain Pygmy-possums gorge on food before they settle into hibernation, but all those months without a decent feed takes a toll – they lose almost half their body weight over that period. The males need to build themselves back up so they are strong and ready to mate when the females emerge two weeks later.

If you were there, you'd see the hungry males scampering among the boulders intently looking for something: bogong moths. Brown-speckled and about the size of a large paper clip, they would have just arrived from their hatching grounds in the lowlands of Queensland, New South Wales and Victoria. After emerging from their pupae, some of them fly as much as 1000 kilometres to reach the boulder fields and caves in the Alps, where they wait out the spring and summer before returning home to breed.

In a good year, more than four billion come, and it's not just Mountain Pygmy-possums that have traditionally feasted on them. For thousands of years Indigenous Australians roasted the moths in hot ashes and mashed the bodies to make nutritious, nutty-tasting 'moth meat'. To the possums, the moths are a vital part of getting ready for spring breeding. But unfortunately in 2017 and 2018, the moths failed to show up, probably because of a major drought in New South Wales and Queensland where the moth grubs develop.

Instead of billions, only a tiny number arrived.

THE WOOD-SHAVING TRICK

Saving an entire species involves lots of expertise and high-tech equipment. But there's always room for simple, yet clever ideas too. The Mountain Pygmy-possums at Healesville Sanctuary need to hibernate over the winter. To accommodate them, they are provided with a climate-controlled facility using the latest technology. But to tell if they are ready to hibernate, the keepers use something available at any pet store: wood shavings. One piece is placed carefully on each possum; if it has fallen off at the next check, the keepers know they have a restless possum that might need more food before full hibernation.

In some caves where there are usually tens of millions of moths lining the walls, there was only bare rock. As a result, the females were unable to get enough food to feed their young. In the spring of 2018, in the worst-affected population 95 per cent of surveyed females lost their young. With only an estimated 2000

Mountain Pygmy-possums left in the world, this is a very serious issue. It was the worst year on record. To try to help the maximum number of moths reach their destinations, the zoo asked everyone living along the bogong moth's migration path to help by turning off outside lights at night to avoid distracting the furry navigators from their southerly destinations in the high plains, and using the Moth Tracker app to report sightings.

But climate change poses other dangers for the Mountain Pygmy-possums too. Scientists warn that over the next 30 to 70 years Australia's alpine regions will undergo major changes. The area covered by snow in winter is likely to shrink, and winters are likely to become shorter, producing less snow. This is very bad news for the possums, first because they will have even less suitable habitat to live in, and second because a shorter winter means they are likely to emerge from hibernation early, before the all-important moths have arrived. Hotter summer temperatures in the mountains are also a serious concern, because the possums quickly become dangerously ill if the temperature gets above 30°C.

With so many challenges to their survival in the wild, captive breeding programs are also very important. Healesville Sanctuary had previously succeeded in breeding captive-born Mountain Pygmy-possums but hadn't been able to achieve the same results with possums caught in the wild, which is necessary to ensure genetic diversity. That all changed in January 2019, when all the hard work by the keepers and scientists was rewarded by seven twitching pink noses emerging from the pouches of their wild-caught mothers, Bev and Plum.

There were celebrations right around Australia at that wonderful news. Those beautiful little joeys were the result of 11 years of dedicated and patient observation and experimentation, giving hope to everyone who cares about endangered animals.

WHAT CAN I DO TO HELP?

Choose paper wisely to save possum homes: Wipe for Wildlife by asking your family, school and clubs to switch to recycled toilet paper. Reuse scrap paper where you can, and for printers choose either recycled paper or paper that has Forest Stewardship Council (FSC) approval so you know it's ecofriendly.

Support possum conservation organisations: These include Zoos Victoria and Friends of Leadbeater's Possum, who welcome families joining up and coming along to planting days and wildlife walks.

Don't leave lights burning at your mountain lodge: If you happen to be in Mt Kosciuszko National Park in New South Wales – or at Mt Bogong, Mt Higginbotham or Mt Buller in Victoria in spring or summer – don't leave outside lights on at night if you don't have to. The lights attract the bogong moths that Mountain Pygmy-possums rely on for food at that time of year, steering them away from the boulder fields where the hungry possums are waiting.

Use the Moth Tracker app to share your sightings of the Bogong moth.

2

The 'Extinct' Ninjas of the Australian Bush

Eastern Barred Bandicoots

With her apple cheeks and bright-eyed enthusiasm, Dr Amy Coetsee could be mistaken for a student rather than a zoologist who has devoted more than 14 years of her life to studying animals. Back in the United Kingdom where she was born, her first passion was for the weird and wonderful octopus. At the University of Aberdeen she studied the venomous saliva of the curled octopus, which it injects into crustaceans such as crabs. (The saliva turns crab meat into crab soup, so it can be sucked out and gobbled up.) Octopuses may have been her first love but in 2005, after emigrating down under, Amy fell for another weird and wonderful animal unlike anything she had ever encountered – the Eastern Barred Bandicoot. "I just think they're amazing!" she says, beaming.

Eastern Barred Bandicoots are about the size of a large guinea pig, with a striped furry rump, bulging beady black eyes, short front legs for digging and large back feet for hopping. And let's not forget their noses.

"They have this wonderful, twitchy, ice-cream-cone-shaped nose with little whiskers on the end."

For the last 14 years, Amy's been devoted to studying and working with these animals, which are considered 'extinct' in the wild. What does she find so intriguing about these little marsupials? A big part of it is their ninja abilities.

Like most Australian animals, bandicoots are active at night. But as dawn approaches they vanish into thin air. They can't pull the ninja trick octopuses do, when they 'disappear' by matching their body colour and pattern to their surroundings (Amy seems drawn to creatures that can make themselves disappear!), but bandicoots have a secret all of their own. If you could watch one closely without it knowing, you'd discover the trick. Bandicoots quickly dig out a shallow nest in the ground, dive in, curl up and cover themselves over. It might not sound like a superpower, but if you saw it for yourself you'd be just as amazed as Amy still is all these years later.

"Bandicoot nests are so hard to find you could spend

EASTERN BARRED BANDICOOTS: FAST FACTS

They are:

Mammals: The mothers make milk for their babies.

Marsupials: The tiny babies go straight into their mother's pouch after birth and stay there until they are big enough to move around on their own.

Nocturnal: They are active at night.

Their scientific name is: *Perameles gunnii.* The genus name for bandicoots, *Perameles*, is another example of European naturalists using Latin words to name a unique Australian animal after a European one it reminded them of. *Pera* means 'pouch' and *meles* means 'badger', so the word means 'pouched badger', even though bandicoots have no relation to badgers.

There are two distinct sub-species: Mainland Eastern Barred Bandicoots and Tasmanian Eastern Barred Bandicoots.

Their babies are called: joeys.

Their average lifespan is: two to three years in the wild and up to six years in captivity.

The biggest threats they face are: loss of habitat, foxes (on the mainland), and feral cats.

Their conservation status is:
Tasmanian Eastern Barred Bandicoots – Vulnerable
Mainland Eastern Barred Bandicoots – Extinct in the Wild.

days walking around an area where you know they live and you'll never come across a nest," she says.

Radio receivers can track animals fitted with tiny transmitters, revealing just how close to the surface they are: "Once you've pinpointed the location using the radio signal, if you look carefully you can sometimes actually see the top layer of grass moving up and down as the bandicoot below is breathing." But without a transmitter these clever little creatures stay invisible in their nests. "Even keepers who work with them all the time can't spot them in enclosures that mimic their natural habitat. The keepers sometimes have to get on their hands and knees and crawl along in a line to find where the nest is!" explains Amy.

When they are calm and feeling unthreatened, bandicoots hop along close to the ground, pushing off with their strong hind legs just hard enough to move forward a little at a time. But when they sense danger, including the hiking boot of an approaching scientist, they unveil their second ninja power.

On average, an adult bandicoot is only around 14 centimetres tall but they are capable of leaping 1.2 metres in the air. That would be equivalent to you jumping, ninja-style, up onto the roof of a three-storey building! If you ever want to test how fast the human heart can beat, try having a ninja bandicoot jump up from the place you were just about to step!

There's also a third ninja behaviour that bandicoots show, but not to their keepers. It's their warrior nature.

"They are the calmest, most placid little animal that you can handle," says Amy. "They just sit in your hand, they don't even wriggle, really. They're so calm I've let my young sons handle them and it's been fine. But," her eyes widen and she leans forward, "they're horrible to each other. Horrible! When you catch them in the wild they might have tails missing, or ears shredded, or places where their fur has been pulled out. I've caught bandicoots that have only recently had their tail fully ripped off by another bandicoot, leaving the bone exposed."

How does she know it's bandicoots doing this to one another and not predators? "Because predators would inflict different injuries – think sharp teeth and claws. You know when you've caught a young boy because he's got perfect pretty little ears. When you've caught an old boy, he's got really gnarly ears. Sometimes females have injuries too but it's mostly males. They are fighting for the females."

They may be ninja warriors, but their superpowers have not protected the Eastern Barred Bandicoots from extinction on the Australian mainland. (Their close cousins, a sub-species called *Perameles gunnii gunnii*, have survived in Tasmania.)

For thousands of years before European settlement, bandicoots were plentiful in the grasslands and woodlands stretching from Melbourne all the way into South Australia. But over the past 200 years, more than 99 per cent of their natural habitat has been cleared for cities and agriculture.

The colonial settlers also introduced foxes. Sadly, the bandicoots' disappearing power was no match for the foxes' sense of smell. The absence of foxes in Tasmania is one reason why the bandicoots have managed to hang in there.

By 1988 just one small group of Eastern Barred Bandicoots remained on the Australian mainland. They were living in the rusted-out wreck of an old Holden car in a rubbish tip in Hamilton in western Victoria.

Forty animals were captured from Hamilton and in 1991 Zoos Victoria created a captive breeding program. Only 23 of the captured animals bred successfully but that was enough to get things going. The program has now produced more than 950 bandicoots. They have been released into different sites, each protected from predators, to allow the animals to thrive.

Some are on islands – Churchill Island, Phillip Island and French Island – which are free of foxes. On the mainland, bandicoot reserves are protected by predator-proof fences. These include Victoria's Mt Rothwell Conservation and Research Centre, Woodlands Historic Park and Hamilton Community Parklands. Because these reserves are protected by fences, even though the bandicoots appear to be living in the bush, they are considered captive and therefore 'extinct in the wild' on the mainland.

But in their protected reserves, the bandicoots are making a successful comeback thanks to even more of their special superpowers. They hold the title of being one of the fastest breeding mammals on the planet. The time it takes for babies to develop inside the mother's womb is just 12.5 days. They can have up to four at a time, and as soon as one set of joeys leaves the pouch the mother can have another, breeding all year round.

It also helps that they're not fussy eaters. "They're like a dream child, really, they'll eat anything," says Amy. In cooler months, when the soil is softer, they dig ice-cream-cone-shaped holes that match the shape of their nose. They are looking for worms and beetle grubs, but they'll eat any insect they come across. "On Churchill Island they've even started eating whole tiny crabs. They're not picky at all!" Over summer they tend to forage on the surface, catching crickets, moths and anything else that's flying around at night. They also eat their greens – vegetables like onion-grass bulbs, says Amy.

Due to the speed with which they reproduce, the total population of Eastern Barred Bandicoots across

FOXES IN AUSTRALIA ARE FERAL, NOT FANTASTIC

Foxes are fantastic in the parts of the world that are their native habitat. And it's amazing how much of the world that is. The red fox – familiar from Aesop's fables and Roald Dahl novels – has the largest native distribution of any mammal other than human beings! It is found in Europe, North America, the non-tropical parts of Asia and the northern part of Africa. But the fox is not native to Australia. It was imported in the 1840s, and released into the bush so that fox hunters could pursue the sport they enjoyed back in England. It didn't take long for foxes to spread across the whole mainland, except for the tropical far north. Because they'll eat anything from native birds and small animals (including farm animals such as lambs) to insects, fruit and garbage, the country was like a gigantic fox all-you-can-eat buffet!

Many native species didn't stand a chance. As Christopher Johnson, Professor of Wildlife Conservation at the University of Tasmania, says, "The red fox may be the most destructive species ever introduced to Australia." Foxes are one of the major reasons for the extinction or near-extinction of many species of mammals, including bilbies, quolls and bandicoots, ground-nesting birds such as the Night Parrot, and even the Green Turtle. The Bass Strait prevented foxes from reaching Tasmania on their own, but in the 1990s someone decided to illegally release them there. The state government established a 10-year eradication program, which seems to have been successful: no foxes have been found in Tasmania since 2011. But elsewhere, federal and state governments spend hundreds of millions of dollars each year trying to eradicate these introduced pests through poison baiting and offering bounties to licensed shooters. Conservationists rely on fox-proof fencing to try to keep endangered animals such as the Eastern Barred Bandicoot safe.

the release sites is now more than 1200, about halfway to the target number for the National Recovery Plan.

While foxes are bandicoot enemy number one, number two is feral cats. When bandicoots were released onto Phillip Island, researchers were anxious because there were feral cats in the area. Although efforts were in place to control the cats, Rachel Taylor, a university student who was working with Amy, decided to see if Eastern Barred Bandicoots could be trained to avoid them.

Rachel designed an experiment that exposed half of the bandicoots released on the island to the smell of cat urine and body odour. They were very interested. So she set up a 'scare' for them – a garbage bin lid with a motion-detector that would pop up whenever they got close to the cat odours but not to other smells, such as lemon juice. They quickly associated the cat smells with the scare and learned to avoid them. Another group of animals received no training. Because the animals were all tagged, Rachel could track their progress.

There wasn't a noticeable difference between the survival rates of the trained bandicoots compared to the untrained ones, but the reason was a happy one – the survival rate of both groups was high.

Bandicoots (and many other native Australian species) are such easy pickings for foxes and feral cats because they evolved to deal with a completely different type of predator: Boobook Owls and other birds of prey. These birds have amazing vision (eagles, for example, can see an ant crawling on the ground from the top of a 10-storey building – you can read more about this in Chapter 6). But this incredible vision relies on detecting motion, so the best way for a small animal to escape is to freeze. A bandicoot standing as still as a statue is pretty much invisible to a bird of prey. Unfortunately, this is exactly the wrong tactic to adopt if you're being hunted by a fox or cat. A bandicoot that freezes when stalked by one of these introduced, land-based hunters has almost no chance of escape.

Amy says while it's possible to train bandicoots to be more cautious and alert when they can smell cats, that doesn't necessarily mean it would help them as a species. "If you train the animals in captivity to [be cautious around mammal predators] and then release them, will they then pass that information on to their young?" she wonders. "We don't know."

But unknowns are okay. Conservation scientists are trying to find the answers. It's all about observing, experimenting, analysing and learning.

Another of the experiments being conducted to try to keep Eastern Barred Bandicoots safe from foxes involves Maremma dogs. If you've seen the 2015 movie

FERAL CATS AND THE 'TOXO' THREAT

There are three kinds of cats in Australia: domestic cats (pets that are cared for and loved); strays (cats that have been abandoned or become lost, and survive by roaming around and scavenging human food and rubbish); and feral cats (that live wild with no help from humans and often have no contact with them). They're all the same species, but feral cats, which may be descended from many generations of feral animals, are often far bigger than domestic cats, carrying up to nine kilograms of formidable muscle. There are believed to be between two million and six million feral cats in Australia, spread across 99.8 per cent of the continent. Their skill at hunting defenceless native animals means they are a huge problem. A recent study in the journal *Biological Conservation* estimated that feral cats kill more than one million birds, one million reptiles and one million small mammals in Australia … not every year or even every week, but every single day. That's more than 2000 native creatures every minute.

Feral cats are a very big danger as predators, but they are also dangerous because of the diseases they carry and spread. The contagious infection toxoplasmosis is of particular concern to marsupials, which seem to be especially susceptible to it. The parasites that cause the infection enter the soil when an infected cat poos there and stay long after the poo has dried up and disappeared. In fact, the parasites can live in moist soil for more than a year, just waiting to be picked up by a foraging native animal. (Humans can easily catch the disease too, so you should always wear gloves when coming into contact with soil, for instance when you're gardening.) And while cats can carry the 'toxo' parasites without becoming sick, contact is almost always fatal for bandicoots.

Oddball, you've probably already fallen for these fluffy big white dogs, which were originally bred to guard sheep in the mountains of Italy. The movie was based on a real-life experiment using Maremma dogs, including the real Oddball, to protect breeding penguins on Middle Island near the town of Warrnambool on the southwest Victorian coast. It was such a success that the program is still going strong 13 years later. Dave Williams, who trained the Maremmas to protect these penguins, is now turning his talents to finding out if they can also help Eastern Barred Bandicoots.

Maremmas are used to protecting flocks of animals, usually sheep, so the idea of them shepherding a penguin colony wasn't such a huge stretch. But bandicoots are a different story. They don't flock; they're solitary. They also pull that ninja disappearing trick during the day. That makes it very hard to get the dogs interested in them. So Dave came up with another plan. The dogs are trained in the usual way that they would have been in Italy, by raising them from puppyhood with small flocks of sheep. But the land they're on is bandicoot habitat. The idea is that if the dogs protect the sheep in the area, the bandicoots there will be also be protected.

Of course for the program to work, the dogs have to know to leave the bandicoots alone. As Amy explains, "They've been trained not to go anywhere near bandicoots. It's amazing to watch a dog wandering around catch the smell of a bandicoot in its nest and straight away move back and walk off in the opposite direction."

Three trial sites using this combination of dogs and sheep are planned, and these will be monitored for two years to assess how successful the experiment has been.

In the meantime, it's clear that the National Recovery Plan is already a success. Bandicoot numbers are looking good at various release sites. And researchers are making sure that they mix the populations to avoid inbreeding – close relatives breeding with each other – which makes populations more susceptible to disease. All the animals are tagged so that researchers can identify them and trace family connections.

Amy says there are lots of reasons to hope that this

fast-breeding and very special little marsupial will survive. “Once you take foxes out of the equation,” she explains, “the bandicoots do the rest. With islands coming on board, we have added thousands of hectares of suitable habitat. We are still a few years away from being able to say we have recovered them and we are not sure at what point we can make that call (you don’t want to do it too early), but the future is looking very bright for the Eastern Barred Bandicoot.”

WHAT CAN I DO TO HELP?

Get behind the rescue efforts: Support Zoos Victoria and other organisations working hard to save the Eastern Barred Bandicoot.

Choose your paper wisely: Wipe for Wildlife by asking your family and school and clubs to switch to recycled toilet paper. Reuse scrap paper where you can, and for printers and other paper requirements choose either recycled paper or paper that has Forest Stewardship Council (FSC) approval so you know it is eco-friendly. Let's not see any more precious wild habitat be cut down for paper we could get from other sources.

Control your cats: Don't let your pet cats run wild, because hunting is instinctive to them no matter how well fed they are. The RSPCA has great tips on keeping cats busy and happy indoors, and creating wildlife-safe ways for them to spend time outdoors.

3

Unique and Mysterious Swimmers

Platypuses

The connection between Dr Jessica Thomas and Millsom, one of Healesville Sanctuary's platypuses, was special right from the beginning. "I met him the first day I started in the platypus section and I thought he had so much personality," Jessica says. She smiles as she describes his antics. "If it's just the two of us, he'll roll over to get a scratch under his bill. He's completely relaxed lying there upside down, to the point where – you know how a dog will chase after you to get another pat? Well, he's like that. If I move my hand away, he'll move his bill over onto it like 'More scratches, please.' But if another keeper comes in, he puts on this bravado, turning over and splashing to show them how tough he is."

This is just one more surprising attribute of a creature that has a long history of surprising us. When Captain John Hunter, the second governor of New South Wales, sent back a platypus pelt (skin) to England

PLATYPUSES: FAST FACTS

They are:

Mammals: The mothers make milk for their babies.

Monotremes: Mothers lay eggs, which they incubate in specially built nursery burrows by curling their bodies tightly around them for up to 10 days. The eggs are not brittle like those of birds, but soft and leathery, like those of reptiles.

Crepuscular: They are most active in the twilight hours at dawn and dusk, but also hunt for food at night and, in some locations, during the day.

The plural of platypus is: platypuses.

Their scientific name is: *Ornithorhynchidae anatinus.* The first word means 'bird snout' and the second means 'duck-like'. Both refer to platypuses' distinctive leathery bill. ('Platypus' means 'flat-footed'.)

Their babies are called: baby platypuses (though some people call them puggles).

Their lifespan: Both in the wild and in captivity they have been known to live past 20.

The biggest threats they face are: pollution of waterways; becoming fatally trapped by rubbish or opera-house yabby nets; land-clearing destroying their burrows; and dog attacks.

Their conservation status is: Near Threatened.

---

in 1798, European scientists were convinced the furry, egg-laying creature – with what looked like a duck's bill, the fur and front feet of an otter and a beaver's tail – was a hoax. Even when taxidermied specimens arrived, this view persisted – many people thought they'd been sewn together from parts of other animals.

But luckily for us the platypus is very real. And each one has its own personality, says Jessica, "Just like humans and our pets, individual platypuses have their likes and dislikes. They've got different food preferences and sleeping habits. The way they each swim is slightly different. I spend more time with these animals than I do with my own family. People say to me, 'How can you tell them apart?' and my answer is, 'A mother can always tell their children apart.' I can look at a photo and tell you exactly which platypus it is by just the way their face looks."

Jessica knew from an early age that she wanted to work with animals – particularly aquatic mammals. "As a teenager I always thought I would be a marine biologist," she explains. "Then when I was at university I found out that most marine biologists study seaweed!" But at uni Jessica also developed a fascination with Australian wildlife, and after completing a master's degree she got her first position at Healesville Sanctuary, working with birds. "That's how you need to start," she says. "You need to be open to working with whatever is available and to get as much experience as you can with lots of different types of animals." A position became available in the platypus section and Jessica clicked with it – and Millsom – instantly. "The more time I spent in the job, the more I realised how little we knew about this animal," she says. "I wanted to know everything I could, so I started my own research project." In her PhD, Jessica tried to answer questions that would improve captive breeding programs for platypuses. She's now one of the country's leading platypus experts.

And Jessica had befriended a very special platypus – Millsom's survival was a world-first. In 2002, his nursery burrow was accidentally smashed by a bulldozer. When the driver saw the exposed burrow, he stopped the big machine and got down on the ground to try to help whatever had been living there. He couldn't find the mother, but he did find two hairless pink babies. Thinking they were rabbits, he took them home to his wife. Fortunately, she took a closer look and guessed they might be baby platypuses. The couple brought the tiny orphans to the Australian Wildlife Health Centre at Healesville.

The Healesville wildlife vets saw at once that these babies were far too young to be on their own. They were just two months old, only halfway through the period during which they are solely dependent on their mother's milk. No one had ever successfully reared such young platypuses and the urgent problem facing the vets was what to feed them.

Zoos and wildlife rescue organisations around Australia turn to a company called Wombaroo when they have to feed orphaned native animals. It supplies specialist animal baby formula for wombats, kangaroos, koalas, possums and echidnas – but not for platypuses, because there has never been enough need for it. Echidnas are platypuses' closest relatives, so the vets tried that formula, but the babies grew weaker and weaker. Desperate for an answer, they rifled through research on Australian animals, poring over the pages, looking for anything that might help. Finally, they found a study that mentioned the chemical composition of echidna milk and how it differed from platypus milk. They then found supplements they could add to the echidna milk so that it delivered the nutrients that the platypuses needed to grow. Sadly, it was too late for Millsom's brother. He had grown too weak and died a few weeks after being brought in.

It was touch-and-go for Millsom too, but eventually he responded to the new milk and started to put on weight. It was slow-going. By the time a male platypus in the wild is 10 months old, he normally weighs around one kilogram. But when Millsom reached that age, he was only about half that. Because of his small size, it would not have been safe to release him back into the wild. Platypuses are very territorial and males can get extremely aggressive with other males during breeding season.

Millsom stayed at Healesville and became so used to humans that his behaviour is very different to what it would be in the wild. One of the most noticeable differences is that he likes to spend a lot of time swimming on the surface. If he had grown up living in a creek or river, he would stay out of sight as much as possible, fearing predators such as eagles, goannas, foxes and dogs.

Being on the surface means he does something pretty amazing for a platypus, as Jessica explains. "I can call him by name and he'll come swimming over to me and let me pick him up."

But despite Millsom's responsiveness and Jessica's many years of experience with handling platypuses, she is always careful when she touches him. This is because, Millsom, like all males, has a strong, sharp spur on the inside of each back ankle. Connected to a venom gland, the spurs can easily pierce the skin and release enough poison to kill a small animal. No human is known to have died from the venom, which platypuses use against other males during the mating season, but those who have been spurred say the pain is excruciating. "So," says Jessica, "even though he is very placid, I do need to be quite careful when I interact with him."

Outside of mating season, Millsom practises his spurring technique on a blue platypus that mysteriously appears in his enclosure from time to time. Don't tell the little guy, but this worthy opponent is something Jessica created from a mop and towel. Platypuses' front feet have claws that are very good for grabbing onto things – including unwanted intruders – and webbing that tucks up behind the claws. When Millsom sees the blue intruder, he uses his webbed paws to paddle over, then grabs it with his front paws and tussles and spurs it into submission. No matter how many times Millsom defeats bluey, he never tires of the game.

Bluey is an important part of looking after Millsom: it's what zookeepers call an 'enrichment object'. Like educational toys for children, enrichment objects pose challenges to overcome, using behaviours the animal would rely on in the wild. They also stop them from getting bored. Keepers put an enormous amount of thought and effort into finding and creating the right kinds of learning toys.

Whether it's a native-grass tussock or a tree-fern trunk of just the right consistency, platypuses have a great time tearing these apart. Occasionally it might be a delicacy such as crickets, but platypuses are more motivated by play toys than edible treats. They delight in chasing a column of air bubbles percolating through their pond, or somersaulting in fast-moving water jets. No matter how old they get, they're always up for a bit of fun.

Take Fleay, for example. (Her name, pronounced 'flay', honours pioneering naturalist and former Sanctuary director David Fleay, who bred the first platypus in captivity back in 1943, a feat not repeated until 1998 and only ever achieved at Healesville and Taronga Zoo in Sydney.) Platypuses are known to live for 20 years, so when Fleay turned 20 Jessica prepared herself to say goodbye. But Fleay lived on, becoming the world's oldest recorded platypus. Jessica says, "Every time she had another birthday, I'd be thinking to myself, 'This is her last year. She's going to get her favourite enrichment items every day.' Normally we try to space them out a bit, but I'd think to myself, 'No, Fleay can have whatever she likes.'"

The gesture was appreciated. "With some of the other animals, I'll think I've found a great enrichment and I'll put it in and they just ignore it and swim off. But whatever I put in Fleay's tank she'd go and play with straight away," says Jessica. "I'd think, 'Thank you! You made the two hours I spent looking for that worthwhile.'" In the spring of 2018 the keeper thought Fleay's time had finally come. "I couldn't see her anywhere. She wasn't in the burrow and she wasn't in the water. I was really worried and ran around looking everywhere. You know what she was doing? Climbing the waterfall in her tank, doing belly whackers into the water. I'd missed her because every time I went around she was up the waterfall running along the top." Two weeks later, Fleay turned 25.

In the wild, there are many things that stop an otherwise healthy platypus living as long as Fleay. Most have something to do with people. Among the worst are rubbish, pollution, yabby nets and discarded fishing gear.

Platypuses eat a lot – they are capable of eating the equivalent of one-fifth of their own body weight each day. Their favourite foods are yabbies, shrimp, insect

ELECTRIC BILLS

When platypuses get old enough to go hunting for themselves, they locate prey using their amazing leathery bills rather than their eyes or nose. Platypus bills have two different kinds of receptors: some that register changes in pressure, and electro-receptors that pick up the tiny electrical charges created by muscle movements in nearby creatures. (Echidnas also have electro-receptors, but while their snouts have up to 2000, platypus bills have 40,000.) Using both types of receptors, a platypus moving along a creek or river bed with its eyes closed can detect the exact location of prey up to 20 centimetres away.

Having nabbed its prey, the platypus stores it in special pouches in its cheeks until it needs to go up for another breath – and while on the surface it quickly chews and swallows the food before diving back down for more. A platypus spends 10 to 12 hours a day foraging, and most of the rest of the time resting in its burrow.

larvae and aquatic worms, but chemical pollution of rivers, creeks and dams can make these species scarce, putting the platypuses at risk of starvation. Plastic pollution can be even deadlier.

Platypuses spend between 30 seconds and two minutes underwater before surfacing to take a breath, then diving down to hunt along the bottom again. With their eyes (and ears and nostrils) closed, they forage with their bills, following the signals being picked up by their unique electro-receptors. They can detect inanimate objects such as logs and walls through their bills, so they don't swim into them, but something small like a plastic bag can be harder for them to spot. If a platypus gets tangled up in a bag sometimes they can struggle free before their air runs out. But all too often they get stuck and drown.

Even something as seemingly harmless as a hair tie can kill. Gerry Ross, manager at the Australian Wildlife Health Centre at Healesville, vividly remembers the day a young platypus was brought in with a hair tie digging in diagonally across her body and into one side of her neck (in the position you would wear a satchel, but far too tight). "She'd probably been hunting for little grubs on the creek floor and got the hair tie stuck over her bill, then tried to scratch it off but instead it's stretched out enough for her to get her front arm through and it's become trapped there," says Gerry.

Shelly, as they named the platypus, was in a very bad way. The hair tie had dug into her neck, causing a wound that had become infected all the way down to the bone. It took more than six months of treatment before Gerry was sure the little creature would make it. "We cleaned and stitched the wound, but you can't keep a platypus out of water because that's where they feed, so the stitched wound was continually breaking down. Almost weekly we had to re-stitch it. There was nothing we could find to effectively cover the wound because platypus fur is incredibly thick, with an underlayer that repels water, and nothing really sticks to it. So it took a long time, but thankfully she did heal eventually."

Closed yabby nets and discarded fishing line and hooks are also deadly. Because yabbies are such a big part of the platypus diet, anything that traps a yabby is very likely to attract the interest of a platypus. One of the most common closed nets is the 'opera house' kind, which rises up into two wings that resemble the sails of Sydney's iconic building. Drawn to the yabbies within, platypuses enter but cannot escape and they drown.

Although opera-house nets have been regulated or banned in some parts of Australia, many people still own them. Sadly, some continue to use them while others have abandoned them in creeks or rivers. And so platypuses continue to die in them, along with turtles and native water rats.

Last year many of Australia's biggest outdoor equipment stores and retail chains announced that they were removing opera-house nets from their stores, explaining the reason to their customers and offering them other, safer designs such as pyramid nets. This was a welcome step for the beloved animal that has pride of place on Australia's 20-cent coin.

Because its image is so familiar, it's easy to take the platypus for granted, but there is still so much left to discover about this mysterious creature. For instance, scientists from the CSIRO recently discovered that platypus milk contains a special antibacterial protein which might one day be used in human medicine.

But it's not easy to learn things about this Australian icon. "One of the big barriers to our knowledge has been that they're just so difficult to study in the wild," explains Jessica. "They're little brown animals that live in brown bodies of water and come out at night, and they're either underwater or underground."

That's why it's only very recently that we've gotten an accurate idea of current platypus numbers, after many groups worked together to track populations for close to 15 years.

The results are concerning. Platypus numbers have dropped by one-third across Australia in the past 200 years. As a result, the International Union for Conservation of Nature (IUCN), the global authority on threatened species, reclassified the species from 'Least Concern' to 'Near Threatened'. Experts will continue to track population numbers, while also identifying threats to the animals' survival and coming up with strategies to help them.

But seeing Millson snuggling up for another cuddle with Jessica gives one hope that this impossible creature will beat the odds, and perhaps we'll solve some more of its mysteries as well.

WHAT CAN I DO TO HELP?

Don't use opera-house yabby nets: Even if you're in an area where these closed traps are not illegal, use open nets, such as pyramid traps, instead.

Always dispose of your rubbish properly: Recycle where you can and secure what's left in a rubbish bin. Even rubber bands and plastic bags can be deadly if they wash or blow into a waterway where platypuses and other animals live.

Switch to phosphate-free cleaning products: Encourage your family to choose wisely to prevent nasty chemicals damaging our creeks, rivers and lakes.

4

Fighting for the Little Guys

Baw Baw Frogs and Corroboree Frogs

If you want to be a zookeeper trying to save Critically Endangered frogs there are some rules you need to follow:

1. No splashing in puddles on the way to work.
2. Look carefully when checking frog ID cards.
3. Be unbelievably patient.
4. It's okay to cry.

Crying is something that Raelene Hobbs has done a fair bit of in her 20 years of frog keeping. But some of the tears have been for joy. Like the time her team found the eggs of a Critically Endangered species in the wild.

Raelene knows that some people find her passion for frogs hard to understand. But that's exactly why she feels so strongly about what she and other amphibian keepers do. "Who's going to fight for the little guys that aren't cute or cuddly?" she asks, her kind, open face unusually serious for a moment. "We have an obligation

BAW BAW FROGS: FAST FACTS

They are:

Amphibians: The young (tadpoles) live in water and have gills. When they develop into adults they live on land and breathe air.

Genus: *Philoria*: This covers six species of Australian native frogs living in mountainous areas in southern Queensland, northern New South Wales and the highlands of Victoria.

Diurnal: They are active during the day.

Their scientific name is: *Philoria frosti*. The *frosti* part sounds like it might refer to the frog's chilly habitat, but actually it comes from the name of the naturalist who first identified them, Charles Frost.

The biggest threats they face are: amphibian chytrid fungus and climate change.

Their conservation status is: Critically Endangered.

to do it because if we don't champion them, no one else will." That's especially true of Baw Baw Frogs. Raelene's grin returns as she says, "I think they're beautiful, but a lot of people wouldn't!"

Close your eyes and picture a storybook frog. The animal in your mind's eye is probably smooth and green. Perhaps you imagine it hopping up to sit sweetly on the palm of your hand. The Baw Baw Frog is nothing like that. Baw Baws are murky brown with yellowy patches on their bumpy skin, they're no bigger than an apricot and they crawl instead of hop. And, unlike most frogs, they love the cold.

They only live in one very specific part of Victoria – the Baw Baw Plateau, an alpine area which is up to 1500 metres high and adjoins Mt Baw Baw, about 120 kilometres from Melbourne. From June to September the plateau is usually covered in snow. Most frogs wouldn't be able to survive in those conditions, but Baw Baws love it.

As tough as they are, Baw Baws are teetering on the edge of extinction. Climate change is partly to blame, because higher temperatures and declining rainfall make it much harder for the frogs to survive and breed.

But the major culprit is a different kind of global menace.

In the 1970s scientists were alarmed to discover that frogs all around the world were dying off. It wasn't just scary for frogs. Frogs take in oxygen, water and chemicals through their moist, delicate skin. Was there something toxic in our air and water? If it was killing frogs, what would it do to us? Or perhaps it was something to do with the warming climate? There were many theories. In 1997, Lee Berger, an Australian PhD student at James Cook University in Townsville, nailed the culprit. It was a fungus that grew in the frogs' skin, stopping them from getting the oxygen, water and salts they needed from their environment. Deprived of these essentials, the frogs typically died of a heart attack.

The fungus is called the amphibian chytrid (pronounced 'kitrid') fungus. It originated in frogs from Asia, and the pet trade spread the disease to countries all around the world, including Australia. So far, the deadly fungus has led to the extinction of 90 species of frogs, toads and other amphibians.

One reason why the fungus is so dangerous to

Baw Baw Frogs is that it thrives in cold conditions. It spreads by direct contact between animals, but more worryingly it also spreads in ponds and streams. When an infected frog hops in for swim, it leaves behind spores which infect the next frog. Spores can also be transported by a person who gets an infected droplet on their shoes or clothing.

That's why people working with endangered frogs don't splash in puddles. It's also why they cover up before they enter the special 'bio-secure' buildings where these frogs are kept. Natasha Rose is a frog-keeper at Healesville Sanctuary. Tash, as her friends call her, says, "Everything in there has been sterilised in some way, and that includes the keepers. I always wear a clean uniform, and if it's a rainy day I wear a whole rain suit on my way to the building so I make sure my clothing stays clean and dry. I take off my boots outside the door and put on new boots that are kept inside. I disinfect my hands, put on a protective gown that covers my whole body and wear gloves in there at all times."

Baw Baw Frogs are incredibly hard to spot in the wild because they live in rugged bushland up to a metre below the surface, amid the leaf-litter and mud. The only way experts can figure out how many there are is to listen to their calls. The problem is that only the male frogs call, and they only do so during mating season, which runs for about six weeks.

What would a world without frogs be like? "Boring!" says frog expert Raelene Hobbs. "And without frogs to eat them, there would be a lot more bugs."

For a long time, no one was sure how many Baw Baw Frogs there were – the best estimate by experienced researchers in the mid-1990s was that there were more than 10,000 adult males and an unknown number of females. In just 20 years, that number has fallen by more than 90 per cent, leaving no more than 500 surviving males. Without urgent help, scientists think Baw Baws will be extinct in the wild in just a few years.

Raelene is one of many people who have been working extremely hard since 2011 trying to save these little frogs. It's been a roller-coaster ride, because there was so much to learn. During her first year she was part of the small team of field specialists and biologists who spent six weeks on Baw Baw Plateau during mating season, scrambling over tree roots, climbing up ridges and sliding down muddy gullies looking for eggs. They had to do this by listening for the call of male frogs and then searching the area around where they thought the call was coming from.

The eggs are in a jelly-like mass and they're extremely hard to find because they could be fairly close to the surface or deep down in a gap in the soil. You have to dig to see if there's something there. But with every handful of dirt you move, you risk damaging or even destroying the prize you're seeking. It's a daunting task, and at first the team on the plateau went day after day without finding anything. It was easy to feel discouraged. As they neared the end of their sixth and final week, they still hadn't found anything. But just before they were due to head back home, while they were checking one of the very last sites they'd targeted, they finally found a batch of eggs.

"Oh, that was crazy," says Raelene. "We were cheering and jumping around with excitement. It was just amazing."

But no one had ever hatched Baw Baw Frog eggs in a zoo before. The keepers had hardly any information to go on when it came to figuring out what temperature the eggs should be kept at and what conditions they would need when they developed into tadpoles.

Unfortunately, the eggs overheated and didn't develop properly. With help and advice from Taronga Zoo in Sydney and the Amphibian Research Centre, Raelene and a team including experts Damian Goodall and Deon Gilbert got 15 of them through to tadpole stage, but only eight of those became metamorphs, which is what they're called when they grow legs and lose their tails. And then, one by one, they began to die.

Almost three months after the wonderful day the eggs were found, Raelene had to phone the head of Zoos Victoria, Jenny Gray, and the Director of Wildlife Conservation and Science to tell them the last metamorph was dead. All three wept.

The next year the team went back to Mt Baw Baw and spent another six weeks searching for eggs, but this time they didn't find any at all. Another whole year passed as they tried to wait patiently for mating season so they could try again.

Finally, in the third year, they had success! They found two egg masses and brought them back to Melbourne Zoo. These produced more than 100 tadpoles, which successfully grew into metamorphs and froglets.

But it was like working through a maths textbook – every time they solved one problem there was another one waiting for them. Once they got baby frogs, the next problem was: what does a baby frog eat?

No one had the answer. The keepers knew adult frogs eat mainly worms, but what did the tiny babies eat? They experimented with all kinds of things. They tried termites but these didn't seem to work: they watched more of the precious frogs die. They realised too late that the problem was brown house spiders. The spiders had snuck into the carefully maintained frog enclosures with the logs and twigs, and eaten the bugs meant for the frogs.

Finally, after much trial and error, the keepers learned that springtails and woodlice are perfect baby Baw Baw food because they are small enough for them to eat and they stay active in the frogs' preferred chilly temperatures of between 2°C and 8°C.

But even though they had succeeded in raising frogs from wild-caught eggs, the number of live frogs was too low. They needed to multiply them in captivity. So when the next breeding season came around, they were back at Mt Baw Baw and managed to find 13 adult males. Finding females was tougher because they don't call.

Deon ("genius that he is," says Raelene) came up with the idea of creating 'pitfall traps'. He and the other researchers dug holes and placed buckets in the ground near to where males often staged their performance. Then they used mesh and sticks to build an ankle-height fence running along from the spot where they guessed females, drawn by the calls, might emerge. The males were on the other side and even though the fence was very low, it prevented the females from getting across because Baw Baws can't jump. Instead they would try to make their way to the males by following the barrier along, looking for a gap. This would lead them to the buckets. They would fall in and stay there safely until the team came to retrieve them.

The idea made sense on paper, but there was no way

of knowing if it would work in real life. Still, there was only one way to find out, so they created a whole series of pitfall traps. "We all wanted it to work," says Raelene, "but even Deon had a little tear in his eye when he found the first female. It was such a huge breakthrough. We thought, 'Wow, we might really be able to do this thing that no one's ever done before!'"

In the end, the traps succeeded beyond the experts' wildest dreams and 11 of the elusive females were brought back to the zoo. In the newly built Baw Baw bunker, these frogs successfully mated and produced eggs. Five long years later, in 2018, the frogs that grew from those eggs mated and produced eggs of their own.

Now that Melbourne Zoo has an insurance population of more than 300 Baw Baw Frogs, they have enough knowledge to successfully breed and grow Baw Baws, and they have placed captive-bred eggs into a chytrid fungus–free gully in the Baw Baws' natural habitat to boost the wild population. It's been a mammoth effort and it's not over yet, but so far the results are hopeful.

Rachel says the progress they've made proves how important it is to remain optimistic. "If we don't get it right, the species will go extinct. So it is a heavy burden on our shoulders, but look where we're at now. It's amazing." Raelene agrees: "If we'd waited, Baw Baw Frogs would have become extinct. It's unbelievable when you think where we were when we started. I would never in a million years have thought that by now we'd be opening the door and hearing healthy males going off their head calling for mates. It all comes down to people saying, 'We're not giving up on this species.'"

*

Raelene might have to work hard to win people over to the motley brown Baw Baw Frog, but it's not hard to find fans of the Corroboree Frog. They are show-stoppers. As their name suggests, they look like they're decorated for a corroboree – an Aboriginal Australian dance ceremony. Their tiny grape-sized bodies appear painted with squiggly glossy black stripes, on a bright yellow body in the case of the Southern Corroboree Frog, or a more greeny-yellow coloured body in the case of the Northern Corroboree Frog. Both of these dazzlers live in alpine areas.

BECOMING A KEEPER: TASH'S STORY

Like many zookeepers, Tash has worked with several different species. She first worked with kangaroos and koalas, then nocturnal animals and native possums, before moving to amphibians. She says, "I think every single keeper has their own approach and their own skills. One of the things I have is attention to detail."

Her career began when she volunteered at a private wildlife park a couple of years after finishing school. "I always loved animals and always loved nature. Volunteering in that zoo environment, I had a classic lightbulb moment. I enjoyed every aspect of the day, I was happy to go to work. I knew it was what I wanted to do. It's an incredibly rewarding job. I enjoy being outside, being physical and caring for the animals, and I enjoy discussing conservation with people and inspiring them to make changes for conservation in their own life. Kids especially are great ambassadors for wildlife and making changes to protect endangered species."

CORROBOREE FROGS: FAST FACTS

They are:
Amphibians: The young (tadpoles) live in water and have gills. When they develop into adults they live on land and breathe air.

Genus: *Pseudophryne*. This covers 13 species of Australian native frogs, although most of the others are referred to as 'toadlets' because of their warty appearance: *Pseudo* means imitation and *phryne* means 'toad'.

There are two types of Corroboree Frogs:
Northern Corroboree Frogs' scientific name is:
Pseudophryne pengilleyi.

The biggest threats they face are: amphibian chytrid fungus and climate change.

Their conservation status is: Endangered.

Southern Corroboree Frogs' scientific name is:
Pseudophryne corroboree.

The biggest threats they face are: amphibian chytrid fungus and climate change.

Their conservation status is: Critically Endangered.

Every individual's markings are different, just like zebras' stripes. In zoos, keepers tell them apart by their photo ID. Still, it's an acquired skill to spot the differences. Occasionally the keepers will nickname individual frogs. Tash, who has been a zookeeper for more than a decade, says, "We did have one we called Prince Charming because he was quite good with the females."

The keepers wear gloves when handling Corroboree Frogs – the bright colours on their skin are a warning to potential predators that they are toxic to eat. Other species, such as South American Poison Dart Frogs, eat poisonous insects to build up the poison on their skin; Corroboree Frogs make their toxins all by themselves.

But having toxic skin hasn't protected them from the amphibian chytrid fungus.

The Northern Corroboree Frog is Endangered and the Southern Corroboree Frog is Critically Endangered. It is even closer to extinction than the Baw Baw, with fewer than 50 left in the wild. Besides amphibian chytrid fungus, the warming climate has altered their alpine habitat, drying out their ponds and killing off plant life, making it much harder for eggs to make it to tadpoles, and for tadpoles to survive long enough to grow into frogs.

Corroboree Frogs in captivity can tell when it's feeding time. Their tiny toes start to wiggle. Tash says it's something they do in the wild to attract crickets. It gives them a very cute look, like someone at the dinner table wriggling with happy anticipation at the thought of their favourite meal. Tash has actually had a Corroboree Frog climb across its enclosure when it saw her come in. She says, "It was like 'Are you going to feed me?' I never thought I'd see that kind of recognition in an amphibian, but it happened."

With numbers so very low in the wild, a captive breeding program is the only way to prevent their extinction. Zoos Victoria began such a program in 2001. Five years after they started trying to raise tadpoles, they had their first successful breeding in 2006. It was much easier than breeding Baw Baws. They only had one male and two females in captivity at the time, and when Raelene first saw the small black-and-white eggs she thought they must be slug eggs. She couldn't believe the frogs would be so obliging. They produced 46 eggs in that first batch; Zoos Victoria now produces more than 2000 a season.

A lot of attention is paid to which frogs are allowed to breed together. It's important to prevent close cousins from pairing up, because they are likely to inherit the same faulty genes.

Some of the healthy eggs that are produced are raised in captivity as an insurance population. Others are taken back out to the wild. For Southern Corroboree Frogs, that means you need a helicopter. "Who would have thought that being a frog keeper would get you a ride in a helicopter to these beautiful remote mountain areas?" exclaims Tash.

The eggs come from the breeding populations at Melbourne Zoo, Healesville Sanctuary and Taronga Zoo. They are separated into groups of 50, packed with sphagnum moss in takeaway food containers that have ventilation holes poked into the lids. The containers are then packed into Styrofoam boxes for the trip in the chopper. Wearing warm down jackets to protect them from the cold autumn air, the keepers stow their precious cargo and climb aboard.

They land a short walk away from tubs the size of

a toddler's backyard splash pool. Using plastic spoons, the eggs are carefully scooped one by one into each pond. Filled with disease-free water and nutrients, here the eggs will have everything they need to develop into tadpoles, then froglets.

Then, as if to tuck them in, the ponds are covered with a thick plastic lid for protection. A layer of ice that forms over winter adds an extra cover. When the weather warms up, the frog team will come back, remove the covers and check them. By that time, they expect to see froglets that are about the size of a little fingernail. As they grow up, they crawl out of the tub to live their lives. The researchers hope that they will come back to the breeding ponds as adults. It takes Corroboree Frogs four years to mature and start breeding so, again, everyone involved needs to be patient.

Researchers are hopeful that if they can keep the population numbers up, some individuals will naturally develop resistance to the chytrid fungus. For instance, nine frog species in Panama, South America, have developed resistance. Meanwhile the rest of us need to do what we can to protect their environment – see the box on page 86 to find out how you can do your part.

So how hopeful is Raelene about the future of these little guys? "I'm getting goosebumps just thinking about how far we've come. The right people were in the right positions at the right time – and none of us are going to stop."

Here's to a very froggy future for all of us!

WHAT CAN I DO TO HELP?

Choose environmentally friendly cleaning products: Make sure the laundry detergent, dishwashing detergent, cleaning sprays and fluids your family use are phosphate-free. Phosphates are chemicals that get washed down our drains and end up in creeks and other waterways where they harm frogs and other creatures.

Reduce your carbon footprint: Turn off lights, use power-saver switches on appliances and take public transport instead of driving when you can. Every little bit helps to reduce the speed of global warming, which is a severe threat to the alpine areas where these frogs live.

Support the work of saving these frogs: Saving species is very important work and it costs a lot of money. You can help by supporting Healesville Sanctuary, Melbourne Zoo and Taronga Zoo, which are leading the rescue efforts.

5

Dancing with Devils

Tasmanian Devils

Dr Marissa Parrott was frozen stiff. Since dawn she'd been trekking through the snow-covered forest in the Tarkine area of Tasmania's remote northwest. She and her team were lugging heavy equipment across the rugged landscape to where they had set traps the day before for some very crafty animals – Tasmanian Devils.

When they reached the first trap, things looked promising. The door was closed and the food was missing. But when they peered in, there was no devil to be seen. It was the same story with the second trap. And the third, fourth and fifth ... even with the eighth trap! What was going on? Perhaps someone who didn't understand the researchers' work and thought they were going to mistreat the devils had freed the animals?

Marissa and the team from the Carnivore Conservancy and National Geographic were there to learn more about the devils to help them survive.

The traps were very comfy, and most devils were perfectly content sleeping off a big meal until the researchers arrived to read their microchip tags, weigh them, take blood samples and check the females' pouches. Then the animals were released. They didn't seem to mind being handled; Marissa's team didn't even have to sedate them. (Of course, Marissa and her team are highly trained and skilled; you should never try to touch a devil yourself.) In fact, some devils were so happy with the arrangement, they'd be back inside the traps the very next day. Marissa called these devils 'frequent flyers'.

Since 2015 researchers have been fitting National Geographic 'Crittercams' on these 'frequent flyer' devils. The Crittercam is a tiny camera that fits on a collar around the animal's neck to capture a devil's-eye view of life. The collars were carefully tested at Healesville Sanctuary first, to make sure they didn't bother the devils and that their special 'drop-off' mechanism worked. This meant researchers could pre-set a time and date for the collar to drop off the devil if they didn't catch it again in the meantime. Or, once the researchers were out in the bush, they could transmit a radio signal to unlatch the collar. Then they'd trek out to find the collar and camera, zeroing in on its location using a GPS radio-tracking device.

But when you're dealing with animals as crafty as devils, things don't always go to plan – as Marissa's team discovered on that freezing morning.

They returned the next day, and this time they had more success. As Marissa approached a trap, she heard the sounds of a devil. Although she had trapped devils dozens of times over, she still felt a thrill every time they caught one.

In this case, it turned out to be a devil they knew well – Usher, a big 10-kilogram male. But there was a surprise in store for them when they checked his Crittercam footage. Usher had figured out how to get just far enough into a trap to reach the food while still able to hold the door open with his hind legs or tail so he could back out with his tasty prize. He was a big fellow with an extra-large appetite, so he hadn't just hit up a couple of traps – he had emptied every single one he could find, until finally a trap closed and he settled down to sleep after his enormous meal.

Even though it meant some of their work had gone

TASMANIAN DEVILS: FAST FACTS

They are:

Mammals: The mothers make milk for their babies.

Marsupials: The tiny babies go straight into their mother's pouch after birth and stay there until they are big enough to move around on their own.

Dasyurids: Unlike marsupials such as kangaroos and koalas, they are meat eaters, or carnivores. Devils are the largest surviving carnivorous marsupials in the world.

Nocturnal: They are active at night.

Their scientific name is: *Sarcophilus harrisii*. *Sarcophilus* means 'flesh-loving' and *harrisii* honours naturalist George Harris, the first person to describe them in writing.

Their babies are called: joeys or imps.

Their average lifespan is: five to six years in the wild; seven to eight years in captivity.

The biggest threats they face are: devil facial tumour disease (DFTD) and vehicles.

Their conservation status is: Endangered.

to waste, Marissa and the other researchers couldn't help but admire Usher's ingenuity and laugh about how he had outsmarted them. It gave them a new catchcry too: whenever they discovered an empty closed trap, they would look to the sky and cry, 'Why, Usher, why?!'

It's the devilish cunning that impresses Marissa most. Although Usher's cleverness is hard to beat, she's come across many smart devils in her career. Yet often people are surprised to find Marissa loves these animals so much. Why do they hold such a place in her heart? Well, they remind her of kids in the playground with really loud voices. The ones who seem like trouble at first, but when you get to know them you find out they're really nice – maybe even best friend material. Tasmanian Devils are just like them. The name 'devil' makes people think they're ferocious, but they're actually sweet, smart, shy and all-round adorable. Unless you're another devil who's trying to take food away from them, that is!

Aboriginal Australians, who knew them well, called devils *tardiba* or *purinina*. But when European settlers arrived and heard them in the bush at night, the noise was so strange and spooky they thought it sounded like the shrieks of devils. When they did spot the animals, they saw pointy red ears and what they thought was an aggressive display of razor-sharp teeth. So the name stuck.

We now know that devils' ears go red when they are feeling anxious or threatened. The colour is easy to spot because they don't have much fur on their ears. And the 'gape', as their wide-open mouth is known, isn't a sign of aggression. It means they're feeling threatened.

But even though we understand so much more about them than the European settlers did, the sound of a Tasmanian Devil in full cry can still make the hairs stand up on the back of your neck. That mix of raw scream, fierce growl and outraged grunt is perfect for the soundtrack of a horror movie. But devils also make extremely cute little *grarrf arrf* sounds that most people don't get to hear.

With their bright, inquisitive eyes, soft black fur, shiny black noses and light-coloured snouts, young devils, known as joeys, might remind you of bear cubs at first. But they have a charm all of their own. Joeys are playful and, if they've been raised by humans, cheeky with their human keepers. Joeys that are raised by humans (for example if they have lost their mums) are happy to climb into a lap for a cuddle or a scratch behind the ears before scurrying back down to give a shoelace a curious tug with their teeth. Then they'll scamper off to explore some more. Joeys are really good at climbing trees (something that becomes a lot harder as they get older and heavier) and they love being in water. They splash and play in water, lie in it to cool down on a very hot day and even hold their breath to dive beneath the surface. When they're tired, joeys roll up into a ball of irresistible cuteness that can fit in your cupped hands.

They have a special trick if they want extra attention or if they think their keepers should hurry up a bit with the food – they will sneak up from behind and try to nip an ankle. So anyone who wants to work with them has to learn 'the devil dance': spot them coming and twist around quickly enough so you can put the sole of your shoe up to stop them reaching your ankle.

Devils make great mothers. They generally mate in March, at the beginning of autumn. Afterwards the males head off, and just three weeks later about

30 tiny pink babies the size of grains of rice are born. Only the strongest of the 'pinkies' will survive. As soon as they emerge, they must undertake the long, perilous journey to the pouch, find a teat and latch on. The mother has four teats but usually an average of three pinkies survive.

Those pinkies that manage to latch on grow in the pouch over the next four months. By the end of that time, they are big enough to venture out for a look. Devils' pouches, like those of wombats, face backwards. This allows them to dig without getting dirt in the pouch. When they first venture out of the pouch, the baby devils stay very close to Mum. If she starts moving and they can't scramble back into the pouch in time, they'll just clamber aboard and hang on to her with their teeny-tiny claws.

By about five months they are old enough to be left in devil day care: a den their mother has made for them – usually an old wombat burrow or hollow log she has lined with grass and leaves. Like toddlers, the joeys tumble about, play and sleep while Mum goes off to find food, coming back regularly to give them milk and make sure they are safe. As they grow older, they get bolder and explore more of their surroundings until, at about 10 months, they head off to make their own way in the world.

Marissa has spent more than a decade trying to make sure devils don't become extinct. She's not alone. Around the world, scientists, zookeepers, vets, rangers and their supporters have joined the fight to save the devils from their biggest enemy. The greatest threat to devils is not humans, but a weird kind of cancer that grows on their face and spreads like a virus from devil to devil. It's aptly called devil facial tumour disease (DFTD). (A tumour is a type of cancer that grows as a solid mass.)

The way devils behave causes this disease to spread, but humans are also partially responsible for making them an endangered species. One of the main reasons this cancer has taken hold so strongly is because of what happened all those years ago, after the first settlers arrived in Tasmania and decided devils were their enemy.

The settlers had brought farm animals with them, including chickens and sheep. Now, devils have big appetites – so big they can eat two-fifths of their own

MAINLAND DEVILS

We know from fossils that devils used to live in other parts of Australia, not just Tasmania. But they died out somewhere between 3000 years ago and 500 years ago, probably due to the land becoming drier and the number of dingoes increasing. The devils that were in Tasmania survived because the land there is much greener and dingoes could not get across Bass Strait.

bodyweight in a single meal (although they might not eat again for a couple of days). That would be like you eating an entire bucketful of pasta in one go! And while parents sometimes complain their kids are too fussy about food, no one could ever say that about a devil. They'll eat pretty much anything as long as it's meaty. They do hunt smaller creatures like frogs, birds and lizards, and are even known to successfully hunt larger animals such as possums, wallabies and wombats. However, it's much easier for them to scavenge for animals that are already dead. Devils aren't even a bit picky: they will eat fresh roadkill or even half-rotten diseased corpses. Their sense of smell is incredible: sitting up on their hind legs ('meerkating'), they take a good sniff and can detect a dead kangaroo from kilometres away.

Their short legs might make you think they don't get far, but don't be fooled. They have been recorded travelling over 20 kilometres in one night. And that means that when there is something to scavenge – for instance, a kangaroo that's been hit by a car – devils swarm from all around. When they arrive, there is often a tussle involving some loud screaming, shoving and biting. While the biting generally doesn't cause serious wounds, it does make it very easy for devils to pass on the infectious face cancer.

Then they settle down to devour the kill, eating the whole lot: fur, bones, everything. They can do that because they have amazingly strong jaws.

Adult devils stand just a bit taller than a Staffordshire terrier. Females weigh about the same as a Staffy, but males can weigh twice as much. All devils have incredibly strong jaws. When you compare their bite-strength to their overall size, no other mammal can beat them.

Having such big, strong jaws means they have unusually large heads. In an adult male, it accounts for one-quarter of his bodyweight. (That's an awful lot; your human head is less than one-tenth of your overall bodyweight.) This is why devils sometimes look a bit funny – as if they'd grabbed the wrong-sized head when they were rushing out the door in the morning and now they're stuck with it. It's easy to see where the design for the Looney Tunes cartoon character 'Taz' came from.

Heavy-duty jaws and big heads are great for scavengers but they're not so great for hunting, where you need to be super-fast or super-stealthy to catch your prey. Despite this, whenever the settlers found their chickens and sheep had been killed, they blamed devils. Perhaps the devils did kill some of the chickens, but they certainly didn't kill the sheep – those are too big. It's much more likely that dogs were responsible. But farmers saw the devils feasting on the sheep carcasses and blamed them. So they decided to try to wipe devils out.

From 1830 onwards, rewards were offered for killing devils and for over 100 years they were hunted, trapped, poisoned and shot. The same thing happened

THAT DEVILISH TAZ

The Warner Bros. cartoon character Taz (full name: The Tasmanian Devil) stands upright, gets angry easily, spins like a top, and has brown fur. In other words, he doesn't bear much resemblance to actual devils. But zookeepers say he helps spark interest around the world in the real thing, and sales of Taz toys have helped fund conservation efforts.

to the Tasmanian Tiger, also known as the Thylacine. The populations of both species plummeted until, on a very cold night in 1936, the very last Thylacine, named Benjamin, died in captivity. Overnight, devils took the title of the world's largest carnivorous marsupial.

Suddenly people realised devils might disappear too, and in 1941 a law was finally passed to protect them. Having narrowly escaped extinction, devils gradually bounced back. Their numbers increased across the state and by the mid-1990s there were about 150,000 devils in the wild again.

However, in 1996 a mysterious new enemy emerged. A wildlife photographer was the first to discover it. He'd snapped a picture of a devil on Tasmania's northeast coast and saw a strange growth on its face. No one knew what it was. But more and more devils started showing up with similar growths, and scientists realised they were looking at a bizarre type of cancer. Cancer is not usually contagious, but devil facial tumour disease certainly was. In an alarmingly short time it had spread through almost the entire island.

DFTD was a death sentence. Marissa's face clouds over when she describes the way it works. "The tumours can sometimes grow on other parts of the body, but as the name indicates it's usually around the face. Before long the devils can't see or eat properly, the tumours' growth starts to take all the devil's energy, and generally within three to six months of the first sign of a tumour the devil's organs collapse or it starves to death. It's really, really horrible."

Infectious cancer is extremely rare. Besides devils, it has only been seen in dogs and clams. How can a cancer spread between different individuals? It's a mystery that scientists all around the world are trying to solve. Cells that belong to one animal should be seen as foreign and rejected by the immune system of a different animal. That's why organ transplants are so tricky. For instance, if your kidney was diseased and you needed a donated one, you'd have to use drugs to stop your immune system from rejecting it. (Unless you had an identical twin, in which case your immune system wouldn't be able to tell the difference.)

In the case of the devil, scientists have a theory as to how the cancer developed. Healthy cells obey strict instructions from their genes. Like well-behaved people, they stay in their own territory and do their own thing. But cancer cells develop mutations in their genes and start disobeying the rules. Like an invading army, they spread out to colonise other parts of the body. In the case of the Tasmanian Devils, those mutations allowed them to colonise not just their own bodies but other bodies as well.

But even then the disease might not have had such a devastating effect if it hadn't been for the actions of those early European settlers. They killed so many devils that only a small number was left. When they began to breed, all the members of the new population were quite closely related to each other.

Researchers thought at first that the reason the disease spread so quickly and easily might be because the devils were all close cousins, their immune systems weren't seeing the cancer cells from other devils as different to their own and so weren't fighting them.

But Marissa explains that doesn't appear to be entirely accurate because when researchers did an experiment grafting the skin of one devil to another, it was indeed seen as foreign and rejected. The leading theory now is that the cancer itself has developed genetic mutations that allow it to hide from the devils' immune system.

DFTD spread rapidly and is now found across about 97 per cent of Tasmania, with only the very far southwest and the very far northwest clear of the disease. Over the next few years scientists expect it will reach those areas too.

No one knows for sure how many devils are still out there. Because they are nocturnal and shy and their dens are hard to spot, devils are hard to count in the wild. Wildlife researchers rely on sightings to estimate the population number. In Tasmania as a whole, sightings are down 80 per cent. In other words, if you might once have seen 100 devils in an area each year, now you only see 20. In some places, you'd only see three! That makes them 'functionally extinct in the wild' in some areas, meaning the species cannot play its usual and important role as the top predator in its ecosystem.

When people began to realise how serious DFTD was, the Australian federal government and the Tasmanian state government worked together to set up the Save the Tasmanian Devil Program. There are now hundreds of experts like Marissa working on these important animals and millions more who care and want to help. Their efforts are making a big difference.

Work is being done in three places: in scientific laboratories, in wildlife sanctuaries and zoos, and in the wild.

NO DEVILS = AN ECOSYSTEM OUT OF BALANCE

Devils are a top-order predator, keeping the whole ecosystem healthy. They do this in two ways. First, they keep smaller species under control. Without them, the population of native macropods (pademelons, bettongs, wallabies and other small relatives of the kangaroo) might increase suddenly, resulting in them eating too many plants and leaving no food for other species, which would then start to die off, throwing the whole system out of balance.

Second, they keep non-native predators like foxes and feral cats away. Scientists believe the reason Tasmania doesn't have a problem with foxes the way mainland Australia does is because the devils have stopped them taking hold. If foxes do get in and start breeding in Tasmania because there aren't devils to stop them, it will be devastating for many smaller native species. Feral cats have become much more active on the island since DFTD arose – they may have already pushed the Endangered New Holland mouse into extinction and Eastern quolls are another target. Once common, the quolls' numbers have dropped by about half and they're now on the endangered species list.

In labs, scientists are trying to learn all they can about the disease to help devils survive it, and are also developing a vaccine-like injection to try to protect them. How do you develop a vaccine against cancer? It's not that different to the vaccine you received against measles when you were a baby. The vaccine was an inactive form of the virus that trained your immune system to recognise and attack the live virus if you ever got it. In the same way, researchers are testing to see whether dead DFTD cells can train the devil immune system to attack the live cancer.

In wildlife sanctuaries and zoos, healthy devils are being kept in captivity as an 'insurance population'. This program started in 2006 and was designed to last at least 50 years, which means that even if things go so badly that all the wild devils die out, the species will not become extinct. So far, the insurance population has about 700 healthy devils.

More than 30 sanctuaries and zoos around Australia are involved, as well as others in New Zealand, Europe and North America. Some, such as Victoria's Healesville Sanctuary and New South Wales' Aussie Ark, don't just have devils in captivity – they've also made big advances in research and breeding them. Working together with the Save the Tasmanian Devil Program, these organisations make sure that the animals are bred in a way that increases their genetic diversity (in other words, there are as few close cousins as possible), giving them the very best chance of survival into the future.

Some of these devils in the insurance program live in two specially created DFTD-free areas in Tasmania. The first is Maria Island, which has never had devils or DFTD, and the second is on the Forestier Peninsula, where diseased devils were removed and a healthy population of devils was reintroduced. A canal and special fences separate this peninsula from the rest of Tasmania and the only access is a via a highway bridge, so wild devils that might be carrying DFTD can be kept out. Both these populations are breeding successfully.

In the wild, rangers and researchers are carefully observing and testing devils to see how they are being affected by DFTD. And recently new hope has emerged. In 2016, researchers reported that a small number of devils in the north of Tasmania may have developed some level of resistance. Normally an infected animal lives for less than 12 months. But the researchers found some infected animals back in their traps, still alive and kicking more than 12 months after contracting the disease. The plan now is to try to find out how the disease resistance or tolerance may work, and then one day breed these special devils and move them as needed to help increase resistance in both captive and wild populations.

But while a glimmer of hope has appeared on the DFTD front, there is another significant threat to devils. The problem is very clear to Marissa and her team when they watch the Crittercam footage. They see a devil wander onto a road and then the headlights of a vehicle bear down on it. Of course, the researchers usually know that that particular devil made it – because they have retrieved its collar. But many devils don't survive. Being hit by cars and trucks is the second biggest cause of devil deaths after DFTD.

There are a few reasons devils are drawn to roads. Their taste for roadkill puts them at risk of becoming roadkill themselves. But devils, like other animals, also use roads because they are easy to walk and run on or alongside.

We can't prevent animals using roads, but we can make it safer for them. One brilliant invention being trialled is virtual road fences. These are posts along the sides of country roads that flash lights and make warning sounds when they detect car headlights. They don't startle drivers, who are warned when they're in use, but they do frighten off animals that might have been about to step onto the road. When the headlights have passed, and it's safe for the animal again, the warning stops. It's a simple but effective solution when used in the correct places.

These fences are being installed in roadkill hotspots. If you live in Tasmania or visit on holiday, you can help figure out where these hotspots are. Download the free Roadkill TAS app developed by the Save the Tasmanian Devil Program. This lets you record where animals have been hit and killed. If a devil is reported as having been hit, someone can go collect the body to be examined for DFTD, as well as to check for any joeys that might have survived.

Devils still have an uphill battle but people like Marissa are never going to give up. "There's nothing else like them in the world. It would be an absolute tragedy to lose them the way we lost the Thylacine. We're not going to let that happen."

WHAT CAN I DO TO HELP?

Spread the word: Tasmanian Devils are unique, they're in trouble and need our help.

Take care on the roads: If you live in Tasmania or visit there on holiday, encourage the adults with you to drive carefully and be aware of animals that might be near roads at night. Ask your parents to download and use the Roadkill TAS app.

Support devil conservation efforts: Saving species is expensive work and donations or efforts to fundraise are always appreciated.

Leadbeater's Possums are sometimes called 'forest fairies'.

The amazing Mountain Pygmy-possums are Critically Endangered.

Eastern Barred Bandicoots are active at night – during the day they 'disappear'.

Platypus Millsom loves his scratches and fighting 'bluey'.

Saving the Baw Baw Frog has been challenging, but there's been great progress.

The bright colours of the Southern Corroboree Frog warn predators away.

Jess, the remarkable, record-setting Wedge-tailed Eagle, was always popular with visitors to Healesville Sanctuary.

Fewer than 30 Orange-bellied Parrots remain in the wild.

Baby wombat Gem was hand-raised after being rescued as an orphan.

Tasmanian Devils enjoy enrichment activities at Healesville Sanctuary – a lot of thought goes into animals' play.

We still have so much to learn about the tiny alpine-dwelling Guthega Skink.

Koalas such as Hazel might look like soft and cuddly toys, but they are surprisingly athletic when they need to be.

Orphaned koala joey Noojee with his wonky nose and his comfort teddy.

Tree-kangaroo joey Kofi explores the world beyond his mother's pouch.

6

Magnificent Birds

Wedge-tailed Eagles,
Helmeted Honeyeaters and
Orange-bellied Parrots

It's almost impossible not to shriek when Australia's largest bird of prey is swooping just over your head, its huge 2.5-metre wingspan momentarily blocking out the sun and its razor-sharp talons passing close enough overhead to cause a breeze that ruffles your hair. But at Healesville Sanctuary one particular Wedge-tailed Eagle was so well-trained that keeper Jason Bell knew he could be trusted to swoop the crowd time after time, before landing easily on a nearby perch, collecting his food reward and then hopping up onto the thick glove protecting Jason's arm from those fierce talons.

The male eagle was called Jess. He was named after the thin leather strap that trained birds of prey have around their ankles so they can be handled more easily: a 'jess'. He and Jason shared a very special bond over 13 years, thrilling hundreds of thousands of visitors at the Sanctuary's Spirits of the Sky show. Jess died in

WEDGE-TAILED EAGLES: FAST FACTS

They are:

Birds: Warm-blooded vertebrates with feathers, wings and a toothless beaked jaw.

Falconiformes: Members of the bird-of-prey family, which includes hawks, falcons, condors, kites and ospreys.

Diurnal: They are active during the day.

Their scientific name is: *Aquila audax*. *Aquila* is Latin for 'eagle' and *audax* is Latin for 'bold'.

There are two sub-species: *Aquila audax* is found throughout the mainland of Australia and in the southern parts of New Guinea; *Aquila audax fleayi* is found only in Tasmania.

Their average lifespan is: up to 25 years in the wild; more than 40 years in captivity.

The biggest threats they face are: loss of habitat, and road trauma.

Their conservation status is:

On the mainland: Least Concern.

In Tasmania: where only around 130 pairs are successfully breeding each season – Endangered.

2018 and even eight months later Jason tears up talking about this very special bird.

But birds weren't Jason's first wildlife passion. "As a kid, I was interested in anything that moved, from bugs through to reptiles. Birds were more of a side interest, but in my early teens I developed a real interest in birds of prey," he says. "I think one of the things that pulled me in was that they were hard to come across, rare to see. When you do start watching them and really see their speed and their power and their agility, all those things put together create a real sense of awe. They're just amazing."

When he became a zookeeper 20 years ago, Jason didn't move straight into working with birds. He first gained experience with other species, including native mammals. After seven years as a keeper, he joined Healesville Sanctuary and it was there that he began working with Jess, who had already been living at Healesville for 30 years.

Way back in 1970, Jess had been found as a fledgling, a bird whose feathers have grown in but is still learning to fly and is too young to fend for itself. Jess's nest had fallen to the ground and he was lucky enough to be found by a man named Graham Carkeek, who had worked at Healesville Sanctuary many years earlier. If Graham hadn't found him, the baby eagle would have died. Luckily for Jess, Graham built a nest for the young bird in his garage and raised him by hand. Two years later, when laws on caring for native wildlife changed, he brought Jess to live at the Sanctuary.

By the time Jason came to work there, Jess had a very mixed reputation. With the keepers he trusted, he was great. Easy to handle and nice to be around. But outside that small circle, says Jason, "he had a reputation as a pretty nasty bird. On occasion he had been known to fly at certain keepers aggressively. That's something we see in eagles, particularly when they have been hand-raised or raised from a very young age with people."

Baby birds go through a crucial stage of development called imprinting – by looking at and listening to their parents, they find out what they are and how to behave. Many animals imprint (for example, in the *Jungle Book* stories, the boy Mowgli sees himself as a wolf after imprinting on the wolves that raised him as a baby) but it's most obvious, and most important, in birds.

Jason explains that birds that are exposed early on to humans instead of their parents, like Jess, become "mal-imprinted: they're not quite sure whether they're people or Wedge-tailed Eagles."

This means they sometimes react to people in the same way they would to other eagles in the wild: "So in a situation where, say, a keeper walked into an area that Jess thought was his territory, he had been known to fly at them and actually hit them, and hit pretty hard too." Normally, in the wild, eagles don't consider people their competition, so they don't do this. It's definitely not something you would want to experience. When they're attacking, raptors (as birds of prey are known) come in feet-first. Aside from the damage those talons could do, being hit by four to five kilograms of Wedge-tailed Eagle travelling at high speed is going to hurt.

Birds have a reputation for not being smart – 'bird brain' is an insult. But many birds have astonishing intelligence. Members of the crow family, for instance, can use tools to crack locks, solve puzzles and recognise individual humans. Eagles are very intelligent too, explains Jason. "Jess could not only recognise faces, he could pick voices and, I'm not exactly sure how, he could also recognise a particular keeper he didn't like from 20 or 30 metres away. I don't know whether it was the jingle of the keeper's particular keys or the pattern of his footsteps, but if we were in the enclosure we always knew when this keeper was making his way down the corridor because Jess would get agitated, calling and bouncing round his aviary and jumping up on the window."

Jason wanted his relationship with Jess to be a positive one. Over the first three months the keeper let the eagle set the pace, waiting patiently for Jess to come to him rather than the other way around. The trust between them built, and after 12 months, their bond was obvious. "It continued to build and deepen over the 13 years we worked together."

Having worked with wildlife for two decades, the keeper has known and cared for many, many birds. Jess, who loved to be scratched on the head and across the back of the shoulders, was, Jason says, "the most trustworthy bird I've ever worked with. A gentle giant." He was remarkably affectionate to Jason and to James Goodridge, another keeper with whom he had a special bond. Jason says, "I'd be in his enclosure,

INCREDIBLE HUNTERS

Wedge-tailed Eagles are carnivores. They will eat dead animals (carrion), with kangaroo roadkill often attracting groups of 20 or more eagles, though only two or three will eat at a time. But most of their food comes from hunting, and they are incredibly good at it. They can reach altitudes of up to 2000 metres and can stay in flight, riding the thermal air currents, for up to 90 minutes.

To us, looking up from the ground, they are just tiny specks in the sky, but their amazing eyesight allows them to clearly see moving prey on the ground from 1500 metres away, and they can see other eagles in the sky up to 4000 metres away. When they have spotted prey, they tuck their wings in and dive at speeds of up to 80 kilometres per hour. But because an object shooting directly down can be spotted by an animal on the ground, the eagles often surprise their prey by diving down to tree-top height some distance away, then coming in fast and low, unseen until it is too late. At up to 5 kilograms, females are about 1 kilogram heavier than males. Eagles are capable of picking up and flying with about half their own bodyweight, and they often take any unfinished food back to a branch in their home tree and store it for later.

They hunt mostly smallish mammals, though they will also eat snakes and lizards. Before colonial settlers arrived they ate native animals including potoroos, bandicoots, bettongs and possums. But then rabbits were introduced and they bred in plague proportions, giving the eagles a plentiful new food source.

The settlers also brought sheep and this created danger for the eagles, which were falsely accused of lamb killings. Farmers were so certain that Wedge-tailed Eagles were killing lambs in large numbers that governments offered bounties for dead eagles, and they were poisoned and shot for decades. The toll was shocking. Almost 150,000 were killed in Western Australia between the 1920s and the 1960s and more than 160,000 in Queensland in the 1950s and '60s. Research by CSIRO scientists revealed the truth: while eagles do eat small numbers of lambs, these are almost always animals that are already dead or ones that are sick and dying. Thankfully, the eagles are now a protected species.

kneeling down cleaning up his poo and he'd come and sit on my foot or almost snuggle up against me. Generally they don't do that. And for most eagles, it would be foolhardy to try and take away food they were clasping in their talons. But I could quite happily walk up to Jess and remove his food and he would just let it go with no argument. He was a really, really gentle and placid bird."

Jess also involved Jason in some special bird activities. Wedge-tailed Eagles mate for life (if you ever see one in the wild, have a careful look around – you'll probably see its mate fairly close by). In the wild, the bonded pair build extraordinary nests, called eyries, together. They generally choose the highest tree in their territory, whether it is dead or alive, and use finger-thick sticks to create a platform in a fork among the branches. Then they gather more and more sticks to build it up. Scientists have found nests as large as 1.8 metres wide and 3 metres deep, weighing 400 kilograms – about the weight of a horse! Funnily enough, having gone to all that trouble to break off suitable sticks and bring them back to the home tree, if eagles drop them during the building process they don't usually fly down to retrieve them: piles of dropped sticks up to 1.8 metres high have been found at the base of their nesting trees.

Jess didn't need a nest because, as a hand-raised bird, he never developed the drive to find a mate to raise babies with. But his instinct for nest building still sometimes kicked in, and when it did he included Jason in the process: "During certain times of the year he would go and collect a stick and bring it back and offer it to me, so I could help build a nest with him. That was a pretty special thing."

On one memorable occasion, Jess was focused on sticks but not, it turned out, for nesting. For a bird that flies freely during shows, there is nothing to stop them flying away forever. But they don't because of their training. "They learn that if they do what we ask them to do, they get something really nice for it. Generally that's food, for most of the birds," says Jason. "They learn that the space they're flying in is a safe, happy place for them. There's no threats and they get all the food they want. And when they come back inside to their enclosure they get an even larger piece of food."

But they are still wild animals with their own impulses. "With Jess, two or three times a year it would get to the point where it was obvious that flying wasn't the main thing he wanted to do, and food wasn't a big motivator for him when that happened," says Jason. "On the odd occasion he'd fly off and I'd have to wait an hour or two for him to decide 'Okay, I'm ready to come back now' before I could get him back in his enclosure."

"There was one particular time when this happened and I was flying him and throwing out food here and there for him, as usual. But no, he wasn't interested. I wasn't quite sure what I was going to do so I watched him for five or 10 minutes up in the trees. I saw he was playing with the branches, trying to break sticks off. I went and found a stick and threw it out, like you would for a dog. He came down, landed, got the stick, brought it back to me and jumped up on my glove. We went back into his aviary and he placed his stick where he wanted it to be placed. That was a pretty interesting day."

With every year that passed, Jess's longevity became more and more remarkable. By September 2016, when the Sanctuary marked his 46th birthday, he was the oldest animal there and was believed to be among the oldest known eagle of any kind. His health was generally good, although he did have a long-running issue with one of his eyes. A growth had been removed from the ridge just above the eye in 2010 and when another lump appeared in the same spot in 2017, it was found to be cancerous. In an astonishing example of the expert care that animals get in world-class zoos, Jess received radiation treatment provided by veterinary ophthalmologist Dr Andrew Turner. Less than two weeks later he was flying in the show again, as good as new.

When he reached 47, the Sanctuary tried to find out if there were any older eagles, but found none anywhere in the world. Healthy and well, Jess continued to perform the starring role in the Spirits of the Sky show, coming out last and drawing *oohs*, *ahhs* and sometimes shrieks as he swooped low over the heads of the seated visitors.

On 12 July 2018, Jess performed two of the flights he normally did during the show. The usual routine was for him to land on a grassy area in front of Jason after each flight and get a reward. "He was standing on the ground and I threw him a piece of food," says Jason.

"He half picked it up and dropped it, which was a bit strange, so I went over and passed it back to him. He dropped it again and I thought, 'Oh, this is something really unusual.'"

Raw with emotion, the keeper continues, "I picked him up and just let him stand up on the glove. But I could feel his legs going from underneath him, he couldn't hold his own weight up." None of the crowd had any idea that anything out of the ordinary was happening because, despite being desperately concerned, Jason simply had to keep talking, trying to get through the presentation.

"I rested Jess's head on my shoulder and instead of trying to fly him home I just walked off with him, giving him a bit of a scratch on the head, and popped him inside. I put him down and went back out to finish the show. As soon as I finished I went back into his room and he was already on his way out." Jason's voice cracks as he relives the scene. "I was trying to give him mouth-to-mouth to try to keep him going but it didn't work. By the time the vets came he had just passed away."

There was comfort in the fact that Jess's passing was so quick and pain-free. "He couldn't have asked for a better death really, doing what he loved to do. And he went so quickly," says Jason. Even so, for many of the people at Healesville it was like losing a staff member.

The Sanctuary is built on land that was previously the Coranderrk Aboriginal Reserve, with 142 hectares of intact ecosystem adjoining the Sanctuary preserved as the Coranderrk Bushland Reserve. It was the perfect location for a solemn and beautiful Indigenous farewell ceremony for Jess. Joining Jason, James and the others who had known Jess in the latter part of his life was retired keeper Kevin Mason, who was working at Healesville when Jess first arrived, and with whom he also had a special connection. "The bonding was so strong I couldn't believe it," Kevin said. "You could go into the enclosure and he would flop on your chest, groom your hair and nibble your ears and talk to you all the time."

Murrundindi is a Wurundjeri elder who opens the Spirits of the Sky show by telling the story of Bunjil, an ancestral being who often took the form of the Wedge-tailed Eagle. He knew Jess well and performed a very moving smoking ceremony for him, then invited the keepers to place a sprig of wattle on Jess's grave, saying,

"This will give him safe journey to the spirit land."

Jess is gone but he is far from forgotten. As Jason explains, he and the others who miss this special bird so deeply have their own way of keeping him in their lives: "We quite often go down to the Coranderrk at lunchtime to sit with him and have a think about things."

*

While Wedge-tailed Eagles have bounced back (at least on the mainland) from the destruction of hundreds of thousands of their kind, other native bird species are in dire trouble. Two of those closest to extinction are the Helmeted Honeyeater and the Orange-bellied Parrot. These beautiful, brightly coloured creatures face different challenges, but in the end it comes down to the same problem: habitat loss.

Extinction in the wild is a certainty for these birds without a major conservation effort. Fortunately, both species are getting that help through National Recovery Plans – while outcomes are far from certain, there is hope. And in each case, the desperate nature of their situation has led to some fascinating lateral-thinking

HELMETED HONEYEATERS: FAST FACTS

They are:

Birds: Warm-blooded vertebrates with feathers, wings and a toothless beaked jaw.

Passeriformes: Birds that perch and, in this case, sing.

Their scientific name is: *Lichenostomus melanops cassidix.* *Lichenostomus* is the name for Australian honeyeaters, *melanops* means 'black', referring to the face markings, and *cassidix* means 'having a helmet'.

Their average lifespan is: four to five years in the wild; up to 21 years in captivity.

The biggest threat they face is: loss of habitat.

Their conservation status is: Critically Endangered.

solutions, which have seen the Honeyeaters given a crash course in Stranger Danger, and the Parrots making their annual migratory flight across Bass Strait without having to lift a feather.

The Helmeted Honeyeater, nicknamed the HeHo, is the only bird that is endemic to Victoria, meaning that is the only place this particular creature lives (it is a sub-species of the Yellow-tufted Honeyeater, which is found all the way down the east coast and into South Australia). In recognition of this unique status, it is the official state bird. But that hasn't been enough to keep it safe.

With its distinctive black face markings and bright yellow crest, this songbird used to be common in swampy forests across a significant area of Victoria. But more and more of its habitat was developed for farms and cities. By 1989, when the Recovery Plan was created, there were only around 60 of the Honeyeaters left, in a tiny patch of forest at Yellingbo (also home to another Endangered animal, the Leadbeater's Possum, which you read about in Chapter 1).

There are now successful breeding programs as well as insurance populations of the HeHos at Taronga Zoo and Healesville Sanctuary. More than one million trees and shrubs have been planted to expand the habitat available to the Honeyeaters, and birds bred in captivity are being released into the wild – after they've had special training, designed to help them survive.

The program is a clever response to earlier releases not succeeding as hoped: fewer than half the birds were surviving one year after release. In fact, many of them had disappeared within a few days of being set free in their new home. Experts quickly realised the Honeyeaters were being taken by other birds, goshawks and sparrowhawks, which are among their natural predators. The conservation team began to wonder if being raised in captivity was preventing the Honeyeaters from recognising the birds of prey as threats. So they created a 'Stranger Danger' predator-recognition experiment to see if they could teach them to do so.

A goshawk, already in residence at Healesville Sanctuary following an injury, was flown outside the Honeyeater's aviary while recordings of Honeyeater alarm calls were played. The experiment seemed to be a great success: when the trained birds were released, 12-month survival rates jumped to 85 per cent. But other things had changed besides the training, including more supplementary food and perhaps fewer predators. So another experiment was undertaken, where half the birds got the training and half didn't. The survival rates for both groups were high – one theory is that trained birds may be training the others.

Using the basic scientific method of testing an idea and measuring the results, experiments are ongoing to try to pin down exactly how much difference the training makes. But in the meantime, the training continues – because anything that *can* be done to help these vulnerable birds *will* be done.

Orange-bellied Parrots, known affectionately as OBPs, are in an even worse state, tragically close to extinction. In fact, with as few as 30 surviving in the wild they can claim the unhappy title of Australia's most endangered bird species.

One of only three migratory parrot species in existence, Orange-bellied Parrots spend the spring and summer in remote southwestern Tasmania, breeding there before flying north to spend the colder months in Victoria's coastal saltmarsh. Their habitat has been

ORANGE-BELLIED PARROTS: FAST FACTS

They are:

Birds: Warm-blooded vertebrates with feathers, wings and a toothless beaked jaw.

Psittaciformes: Members of the parrot family, which also includes parakeets, budgerigars, lorikeets and macaws.

Their scientific name is: *Neophema chrysogaster*. *Neo* means 'new' and *phema* means 'voice', *chryso* means 'golden' and *gaster* means 'belly'.

Their average lifespan is: around 2.5 years in the wild; around 5.5 years in captivity, but up to 14 years has been recorded.

The biggest threat they face is: loss of habitat.

Their conservation status is: Critically Endangered.

reduced and changed due to human development, drought and invasive weeds, and their all-important breeding grounds have shrunk to just one small area in the Melaleuca region.

In order to prevent the OBPs' complete extinction, breeding programs have been set up at wildlife centres in four states, including a Tasmanian government facility in Hobart, Adelaide Zoo, and Healesville Sanctuary. There are now more than 400 birds in total held across these sites. The idea is to maintain insurance populations but also to release captive-bred birds into the wild.

With so few birds now in the wild, those involved in the rescue efforts for the species were very concerned at the prospect of losing even a few individuals during their difficult and dangerous 500-kilometre migration across Bass Strait. Once again, thinking outside the box produced a clever solution: instead of making the birds fly themselves, why not give them an all-expenses-paid trip? Also, instead of simply hoping they would find suitable habitat in which to survive the winter, why not have them safely spend the winter at Werribee Open Range Zoo?

And that is why, in April 2018, 10 parrots were captured at Melaleuca and carefully crated up before being put aboard a small private plane for the trip north. At the end of the winter they were joined by six captive-bred birds and put back in the plane to be taken safely back south again.

Michael Magarth, senior research manager for Zoos Victoria, says, "Obviously it's not going to be sustainable to continue to do this with every bird. But it's being tried just to attempt to give an initial boost to the population, to get it up into the hundreds rather than have another year like 2017 where only 20 birds returned to Melaleuca. It's definitely an unusual conservation action – one brought about by extreme circumstances because this bird really is right on the edge of extinction."

WHAT CAN I DO TO HELP?

Choose paper wisely to save bird homes: Every single day, around 30,000 trees go down the toilet worldwide – chopped down just to make toilet paper. Recycled toilet paper is made from paper that has already been used once, in office printers, in schools and at home. It gets a second life as toilet paper so no more trees have to die for a flush. Wipe for Wildlife and encourage people you know to make the switch.

Take part in the Aussie Backyard Bird Count: Each October, during Bird Week, Australians all around the country are invited to take part in a bird census. It can take as little as 20 minutes of your time and you don't even need an actual backyard. To find out more go to www.aussiebirdcount.org.au or download the free Aussie Bird Count app to find out more.

Control your cat: Protect birds and other native wildlife by not letting your cat roam freely.

Watch for eagles on the road: As well as hunting, Wedge-tailed Eagles scavenge roadkill, making them vulnerable to being hit themselves. Encourage family members in country areas to be wildlife-aware drivers.

7

Rethinking Reptiles

Guthega Skinks

Some people think Peter Comber has drawn the short straw. His job as reptile keeper at Healesville Sanctuary is probably just something he has to put up with until he gets promoted to working with nice furry animals. But Pete sets them straight. "Lots of people screw up their face at the idea of being around reptiles. But this is what I love to do." Of all the animals he could work with – lions, tigers, gorillas or kangaroos – it was reptiles that captured Pete's heart.

Pete is a lizard whisperer. He understands them and is convinced they're far smarter than we give them credit for.

A big man with closely cropped hair and a bushranger's beard, Pete's a gentle giant. His patient, thoughtful manner immediately puts the youngest and shyest zoo visitors at ease.

His interest in 'cold-blooded creatures' began in his grandmother's backyard. "My granny would take

GUTHEGA SKINKS: FAST FACTS

They are:

Reptiles: air-breathing vertebrates with dry, scaly skin.

Skinks: part of a family of more than 1500 species of lizard, with cylindrical bodies and short legs.

Birth: They give birth to live young.

Alpine: They live only at altitudes between 1600 and 2170 metres.

Their scientific name is: *Liopholis guthega. Liopholis* is the name for the skink family of lizards.

Their average lifespan is: estimated to be four to five years in the wild. The oldest Guthega Skinks in captivity are now twice the average age in the wild.

The biggest threats they face are: bushfires and climate change.

Their conservation status is: Endangered.

me and my brother out looking for skinks and frogs. We'd find them and take them home. Nowadays we don't recommend people do that, we want them to stay in their natural environment."

Pete is still fascinated by skinks. These days most of his attention is devoted to the extremely rare and Endangered Guthega Skink. Pale brown-grey with a constellation of creamy spots on its back and sides, it is a close relative of the skinks you see sunning themselves on a garden wall – but with a body that measures around 11 centimetres, it is five times longer.

It also has an amazing superpower. While most lizards thrive on warmth, the Guthega Skink can survive in freezing conditions. It lives high in the Australian Alps, camouflaged on rocks or rustling about in the tussock grassland and heath, lying in wait for insects.

Up above 1600 metres, the winters are brutal, with fierce blizzards and temperatures that can reach nine degrees below zero. The secret to the skinks' survival is similar to that of their neighbours, the Mountain Pygmy-possums (who you read about in Chapter 1). They burrow down under a metre of snow, where the temperature remains one to two degrees above zero. In shared burrows, they stop eating and their body functions gradually shut down. This is called 'brumation', the reptile version of the 'hibernation' that Pygmy-possums are doing nearby.

In true hibernation, the internal systems of certain mammals slow down so much the animal can get through the harshest winters using almost no energy. Their hearts beat so infrequently that they can even seem dead at first. But although the term 'hibernation' is used for a lot of creatures, including bears, they are actually in a state called torpor. It's a very deep sleep but it's not the almost complete system shutdown that true hibernators including bats, hedgehogs and ground squirrels experience. Reptiles in brumation can go months without eating, and their bodies use almost no energy.

There is still so much we don't know about Guthega Skinks, but Pete and the threatened species team at Healesville Sanctuary are finding out more all the time through their skink breeding program. Someone whose work has been invaluable in helping save these little lizards is Zak Atkins, a researcher from La Trobe

University who has spent years studying this fascinating little creature in the wild.

Zak is a cross between tech nerd and cunning hunter. Carefully looking for the tell-tale signs of a burrow entrance, which anyone who hadn't been studying skinks for as long as he has wouldn't even see, he catches the skinks, weighs them and fits them with tiny microchips, like those used to identify cats and dogs but much smaller. The chips allow him to check on the health of the individual skinks over time, recording information including their changing body temperature. Zak's work gives the team at Healesville vital data about skinks that can help them breed a population in captivity to be released into the wild, in case the existing wild Guthega Skinks die out.

One of the biggest immediate threats to Guthega Skinks is bushfires. While fires have been a natural feature of the Alps for thousands of years, they have been infrequent until now. According to one estimate, large fires occurred every 50 to 100 years. This allowed the bush to regenerate and local animal species to bounce back. But climate change is making the fires far more frequent and intense. As skink habitats go

IS IT OKAY TO KEEP REPTILES AS PETS?

A lot of people keep reptiles for pets. But zookeeper Pete Comber wonders whether they should. "I grew up keeping lizards and snakes as pets, and I still have some snakes at home. But I don't think I'll be getting any new ones," he explains. "The more we look into some of the behaviours and cognitive abilities of some of these animals – and I'll include fish in this too – the tougher it gets. I've kept fish for a long time. Right now I don't have any, and I'm really torn. I'd like more, but I know a lot more about fish now and I'm not convinced that I'd be happy looking at fish in a tank and telling myself it was okay."

Pete knows how intelligent and complex these animals are, so he's particularly concerned when people keep fish or reptiles in small tanks.

"I've never liked that, but even less so these days." As Pete explains, it's hard to tell if a pet reptile is happy or not. "Just because a pet snake, for instance, mates and lays eggs at the right time each year, does that make it okay? What's it doing the rest of the time? It's sitting there on the heat pad, or it's sitting there under the hide. Is it happy? We don't know."

Pete knows that many people do still choose to keep reptiles as pets and he has some advice: "If people are going to keep them, I encourage going with really big enclosures. The bigger the better."

up in flames, some skinks perish in the fires and those that survive find their homes have been damaged or destroyed along with the plants, insects and other creatures they need to eat to survive. With fires becoming more frequent, their habitats are not recovering fully before the next fire hits.

The 2003 bushfire that burned through large areas of Kosciuszko National Park destroyed the population of Guthega Skinks at Smiggin Holes. Since then, Guthega Skinks can only be found in two places: high on Mt Kosciuszko, and 100 kilometres to the southwest on the Bogong High Plains, sharing the ski fields of Falls Creek.

As mountain tops warm, more trees will start growing in the tussocky grasslands, making fires even more likely.

Fearing the worst, Zoos Victoria set up the Guthega Skink breeding program at Healesville. But because so little was known about Guthega Skinks at the time, they didn't know how to breed them. Zak's data and the zookeepers' skills would both prove crucial. Pete, for instance, carefully observed his new charges and got to know their differences. "We know which ones are bolder and which are shyer, who's likely to come back out of the burrow within a couple of seconds as opposed to three minutes."

The team knew they would have to replicate the extreme conditions the skinks lived in naturally. Being 'cold-blooded', skinks can't regulate their temperature. During their active months the skinks need places to bask in warmth but also need cooler retreats, as they would have in the wild. Getting the conditions right for brumation was particularly challenging. For instance, how quickly should they thaw them at the end of winter?

One year, three of the five females in the breeding program died during the warm-up. The team had lost the majority of their females without breeding a single lizard. "That was a disaster," says Pete, grimacing at the memory. "We had to try and work out why it happened." It was a big question: The others survived so why did these ones die?

When such events take place, it's not always possible to find out why they happened. But Pete and the team were incredibly lucky to have the help of a German scientist who could read the age of lizard bones. Reptiles do their growing in the spring and summer. A cross-section of their bones reveals the fast and slow growth, just as you can see a tree's growth – and judge its age – from the rings in the trunk. The wider, paler and sparser rings are the fast growth, separated by darker rings that mark their winters. Together, a dark and light band marks a single year, so you can tell the lizard's age by counting the rings.

Zak clipped a tiny toe-bone from each of the dead skinks and sent them to Germany to be analysed. The answer that came back was a huge relief. The keepers had not done anything wrong. The skinks had died of old age. They were all aged seven – well past their average lifespan in the wild, based on Zak's studies.

Zak had even more helpful information from the microchips data he'd collected. The microchips had recorded the skinks' body temperatures for 10 months. When Zak recaptured the skinks and downloaded the data, it showed that their body temperature during brumation averaged just 2°C. But it also showed something unexpected – they did not thaw gradually. They rocketed from 2°C one day to 30°C the next, presumably the result of heading straight from their snow burrow to basking in the warm spring sun.

As Pete explains, before they got this information "we were slowly staggering the warm-up, bringing them up step by step to active or 'operating' temperature". They changed this, mimicking nature by turning the thaw program to rapid and it worked brilliantly. The skinks were able to return to a healthy, active state, and the following March a tiny Guthega Skink was born at Healesville. Unlike some reptiles, who lay eggs, Guthega Skinks give birth to live young. This was the world's first Guthega Skink bred in captivity. After six long years of trying, the team were ecstatic.

"That made our day, our week, our month, made all those years we'd put into trying," says Pete.

The team had known that one of the skinks was pregnant, so they'd been keeping their fingers crossed, but they didn't know when exactly the baby would be born.

The reason for that is to do with warm- versus cold-bloodedness. You'll often hear reptiles referred to as 'cold-blooded'. It's a way of describing how they are different to us, but it's not very accurate. The bodies of humans and other mammals (and birds too) are designed to maintain a fairly constant internal body temperature, no matter how hot or cold it is outside and no matter whether we are still or active. Automatic responses to heat and cold, including sweating and shivering, kick in as the temperature changes, in order to keep our insides at about 37°C. (Of course, pushed too far the system will fail, which is why extreme temperatures can be fatal.)

The internal temperature of reptiles, fish and amphibians is much more variable because they can only control it by taking in heat from the outside environment (sitting in a spot warmed by the sun or another source of heat), or shedding heat by finding shade or an underground shelter.

Pete explains they were expecting the baby to be born a bit earlier than it would have been in the wild "because we provide more consistent conditions in respect to food and temperature. So the young one could develop at a much more consistent, and therefore faster, rate. But it came even earlier than we expected. It was a really nice surprise the day we discovered our tank of two Guthegas had turned into three."

It takes quite a while to be able to identify the sex of a young skink, so at first the keepers didn't know if it was male or female. But that didn't matter in terms of naming because, unlike many other zoo animals, the skinks generally aren't given names. Pete and the others in the team do give them nicknames, though, to make it easier to identify them in conversation. Things like No Toes, Wobbly Girl or Funky Foot. "I'll say something like, 'I didn't see Funky Foot yesterday. I saw a head in the burrow but I don't know if it was her,' and they'll know which one I'm talking about," he explains.

You'll notice there's no mention of tails in these nicknames. That's because tail length isn't a very useful physical identifier of skinks (including the largest member of the family, the Blue-tongue Lizard) because they have the ability to 'drop' their tail. It's a defence mechanism against predators, including birds and snakes. If a predator has them cornered, they will wave or wiggle their tail enticingly in the hope of being bitten or grabbed there rather than elsewhere. If it works, they contract their tail muscles and the tail separates from the body. Stored energy keeps the tail moving long enough to keep the predator busy, giving the skink time to hopefully make its getaway. A new tail grows over time.

Using the tail as an escape tool is impressive enough, but they can do something even niftier than that – they can drop more or less of it, depending where it's been grabbed. This is possible because there are 'fracture planes' along its length, allowing it to break off cleanly in various spots. If a predator is gripping close to the body, the skink will drop the whole tail, but if they are closer to the end, only part of it will drop.

All of this happens in a fraction of a second and it happens instinctively: signals fly along the nervous system to the lizard's brain and the response is triggered. No thinking is required. A lot of people would assume that didn't even need pointing out – after all, reptiles can't actually *think*, can they? All they do is react, right? Maybe you've heard the phrase 'reptilian brain' or 'lizard brain', which people use to mean 'responding without thinking'.

The famous astrophysicist and science communicator Carl Sagan described the human brain as having complex, highly developed parts surrounding a non-thinking, unevolved structure that was "something like a brain of a crocodile". That was almost 40 years ago, but lots of people still believe it. Even psychologists refer to people having 'lizard brains' when they react without thinking. But new research is showing us that we have underestimated what goes on in the brains of reptiles, and fish as well.

Part of what made us assume reptiles couldn't think was the fact that their brains are, proportionately, so much smaller than those of mammals. The brains of snakes account for just 1/1500 of the animal's bodyweight. For cats, it's 1/100 and for humans it's 1/40 – in relation to body size, your brain is more than 37 times as big as a snake's. But new technology has given scientists new insight into reptiles' brains and they've discovered that lizards have complicated brain structures, just as mammals do. That fits with research that shows reptiles can learn to navigate mazes and can solve problems, such as finding a way to access food hidden under differently coloured buttons. In other words, they can think.

For Pete, this all makes sense. "Four separate people who work with crocodiles have told me the crocs can recognise different people. And archerfish – that research is amazing." Archerfish, found in the waters of Australia, Asia and Melanesia, are very cool creatures that catch insects and other small prey by squirting a jet of water out of their mouth to knock their prey down and into the water where they're waiting to swallow it. In a recent study, scientists showed that the archerfish could be trained to pick out a specific human face from a line-up with incredible accuracy.

First of all, the researchers, including Australian scientists, trained the fish to recognise a specific face and spit water at it. They then mixed that face into a group of 44 different faces. But the fish still picked out the right face at least 77 per cent of the time – way higher than is possible through mere chance. A later experiment found the fish could still spot the target face even when it was tilted on an angle or tipped on its side. "It's quite possible that skinks are the same," says Pete. "If archerfish can tell faces apart, why couldn't skinks? We've learnt a lot, but we're realising how much we still have to find out."

But despite everything we've learnt, many people respond to reptiles with either fear or disgust. Pete sees this most frequently with snakes. "I told someone recently that I was going away camping, and before I'd even finished the sentence he said to me, 'Be careful of snakes.'" This person had no idea Pete works with reptiles, but even when people do know they don't hold back. People often tell him about seeing snakes when they were camping or bushwalking.

"They'll say, 'I went over and I donged him a couple of times until I got him.' Then they'll describe the snake: 'It was about this long, and it was this colour. What do you reckon it would have been?' In other words, they had no idea what kind of snake it was, they just saw it and killed it. When I ask them, 'Why did you kill it?', they'll look at me like I was an idiot. 'It's a snake, that's why,' was the answer. They think they're doing the community a service." Pete shakes his head. "I would like to think that attitude is changing, but it's hard to know."

Many of the people who think nothing of killing a snake probably wonder why it matters if the Guthega Skink ceases to exist – it's just one little skink, after all. "Yes," says Pete, "but in the bigger picture it's not just one little skink." If Guthega Skinks die out, it means the ecology of the general area where the skink lives has changed. "It means that there could be further changes that we can't predict and foresee," explains Pete. "If there are animals living there that rely on a Guthega Skink once a week for their food and the Guthegas disappear, they turn their attention to something else, putting greater pressure on that animal. And if the Guthega Skinks aren't there to eat bug X, then bug numbers explode and they start hammering plants A, B, and C, leading to increased erosion."

Pete is describing something that scientists are much more aware of today – that all species in an area are dependent on each other. This is called the 'web of life' or 'biodiversity'. It explains why scientists work hard to save species from extinction. As Pete says, "There are so many things that could happen as a result of one little skink going extinct, and we have no way of knowing what those things might be until it's too late. Let's not let it get to that. Let's fix it while we can."

WHAT CAN I DO TO HELP?

Get behind the rescue efforts: Support Zoos Victoria and other organisations working hard to save the Guthega Skink.

Control your cats: Protect native lizards, including the skinks in your neighbourhood, by not letting cats roam freely. A study in the journal *Wildlife Research* estimated that pet cats kill a shocking 53 million reptiles in Australia each year. The RSPCA has great tips on keeping cats busy and happy indoors, and creating wildlife-safe ways for them to spend time outdoors.

8

Square Poos and Gold-medal Speed

Wombats

Raising an orphaned animal is always a labour of love. Just like tiny human babies, they require lots of tender care, plenty of feeds and a fair bit of cleaning up – even if they are very strong and determined baby wombats. But as Healesville Sanctuary zookeeper Katherine Sarris will tell you, it might be a lot of work, but it can be a lot of fun too.

Hand-rearing lovable baby Southern Hairy-nosed Wombat Gem gave Katherine even more appreciation for these surprising animals, who have gold-medal speed, square poos and backsides so tough they can crush an attacker's skull!

For a while there, it was touch-and-go as to whether the injured six-month-old baby wombat would make it. She was found wandering beside a road. Her mother, in whose pouch she should have been nestled, had presumably been killed by a car. The vet team who cared for Gem had two immediate problems to deal with.

WOMBATS: FAST FACTS

They are:

<u>Mammals</u>: The mothers make milk for their babies.

<u>Marsupials</u>: The tiny babies go straight into their mother's pouch after birth and stay there until they are big enough to move around on their own.

<u>Nocturnal</u>: They are active at night.

There are three surviving wombat species:

<u>The Bare-nosed or Common Wombat</u> (*Vombatus ursinus*), found in Queensland, New South Wales, Victoria, Tasmania and South Australia.

<u>The Southern Hairy-nosed Wombat</u> (*Lasiorhinus latifrons*), the smallest of the three species, found in the dry scrubland and Mallee of South Australia.

<u>The Northern Hairy-nosed Wombat</u> (*Lasiorhinus krefftii*), the largest of the three species, now found only in a tiny fragment of just one national park in Queensland, with fewer than 300 individuals remaining.

Their babies are called: joeys.

Their average lifespan is: 12 to 15 years in the wild, more than 20 in captivity; the oldest recorded individual, Bare-nosed Wombat Patrick, lived to 31 at Ballarat Wildlife Park.

The biggest threats they face are: loss of habitat, and road trauma.

Their conservation status is:
Bare-nosed or Common Wombat – Least Concern;
Southern Hairy-nosed Wombat – Near Threatened;
Northern Hairy-nosed Wombat – Critically Endangered.

The first was the deep wound near her hip.

Treating injuries in wombats is always tricky because they will do everything they can to pull the stitches out. Even if the wound is covered with bandages, they'll tug and roll and scrape and bite away until they get to it. We've all seen sorry-looking dogs and cats wearing stiff plastic cones around their necks to stop them getting at their stitches. Those cones are called Elizabethan collars, because they resemble the neck ruffs worn in the court of Queen Elizabeth I. But

Elizabethan collars don't stand a chance with wombats.

Young wombats like to explore their surroundings – at full speed. That means they often run headfirst into tree-trunks or walls. You'd think it would cause them damage or at the very least hurt them, but wombats have extremely hard heads, "You see them crash into something and think, 'Oh no!' But they're absolutely fine," says Katherine. The baby wombat might be okay, but Elizabethan collars aren't made for that kind of punishment. So keeping Gem's wound clean and making sure it healed was one challenge. Getting Gem to eat was the other.

Wildlife rescue centres have baby wombat formula and use teats specially shaped for different aged joeys. Even so, it often takes a while for the wombat joeys to accept this unfamiliar food. "We have to put them in a blanket and wrap them really tightly to try to get them to drink," says Gerry Ross, who runs the Healesville animal hospital (more formally known as the Australian Wildlife Health Centre). "But once they get onto it, wow, they love it." Luckily, Gem's wound healed well, and as soon as she got used to the bottled formula, she started to thrive.

The little wombat's room at the hospital had bark on the floor and some small logs and branches to make her feel at home. To help her settle, she also had a 'pouch' – a small closed-off soft tunnel designed for a cat to sleep in. It worked really well to give her the secure feeling she would have had in her mother's pouch. Unlike with kangaroos, wombat pouches faces backwards so that dirt isn't flung towards the pouch or into the joey's face when its mum is digging (like Tasmanian Devils, which you read about in Chapter 5). The babies use their paws to spread open the pouch fold, then they walk in. "The little cat tunnel replicated that really well," says Katherine.

Once Gem's wound had been dealt with and she had become used to the formula, Katherine became her carer, which meant taking the little joey home every evening, so she could feed her and care for her overnight, then bring her back again the next morning. At six months, Gem was more or less the shape of an AFL football and the weight of a smallish cat, so Katherine could transport her in a special pack. "I would take the little tunnel that she slept in and put it in the transport pack with some blankets around it. She would walk into the pack and I'd close the door. The vets had given me a supply bag with teats, bottles, sterilising solution just like you'd use for human babies, and a supply of the powdered milk. I'd strap the transport pack into the back seat to keep Gem safe for the ride home."

At home, Katherine had a chew-proof wooden crate, one metre square, with a tough wooden base and interlocking walls made of super-hard wood, with a little gate on one side. Wild wombats prefer to toilet under low-lying shrubs, so Katherine set up a kitty-litter tray filled with bark and mulch, and hung some eucalyptus branches over it. Gem obliged.

Gem needed regular bottle feeding. "She would have one feed in the evening, around 9 pm, and another before I went to work, around 6 am," says Katherine. "You make up the milk like you would with human baby formula, boiling the water then waiting for it to get down to body temperature so it's safe for her to drink. I'd take her out of the crate and let her wander around while I was getting the milk ready, then I'd sit on the ground cross-legged to feed her. In the very early stages I would have her in her tunnel pouch, holding her so she was lying on her belly facing up to the bottle, in the same position she would have been inside her mum's pouch reaching up the teat. As she guzzled the milk down, I could feel her paws kneading, the way she would have kneaded around her mum's teat to keep the milk flowing."

"As she got older, she would climb on my lap and just get herself into position. They say wombat joeys always have a distinct preference for which side they want to drink from, and that was certainly the case with Gem. She always wanted me to hold the bottle on my right side. If I tried with the left, she was clearly uncomfortable."

At every feed, Katherine noted down how much milk Gem had been offered and how much she had drunk. She also weighed her every day.

This was Katherine's first experience hand-raising an animal. Other keepers warned her that because wombats are nocturnal animals, the humans in the house might not get too much sleep as Gem moved about and knocked against the crate. But, says Katherine, "I didn't hear a peep from her. She loved her crate and was always happy to be in there. Some nights

SQUARE POOS, NOT SQUARE BUMS!

Wombats are the only animal in existence whose poo comes out in cubes. Zookeeper Katherine Sarris says one of the questions she gets the most is whether the place where the poo exits is square-shaped. It's not – wombats aren't made of Lego!

So how do you get square poos? In 2018 American researcher Patricia Yang found that wombat intestines have two ridges or grooves running down the sides – imagine a sausage-making machine with square sides. This forces anything that passes through it into a cuboid shape.

Wombats use their poo, or scat, to mark the edges of their territory. One theory is that the square shape stopped it rolling off a log or a boulder, and therefore made a better marker. But wombat expert Mike Swinbourne says that's not so: "It's not like they're trying to build little brick pyramids."

In his view, square poos are more likely a result of the dry environment wombats live in. They need to squeeze every tiny bit of moisture out of their food so it can be absorbed and used by their bodies. They're really good at it too, which means they need almost the least drinking water of any mammal – only about a quarter of that needed by kangaroos, which can cover much more ground searching for a drink. So the wombat's ridged intestine helps to squeeze out all the moisture that's in the food they are digesting, and Mike notes that when they have access to more water, their poos become less square.

after she'd had her feed and before I went to bed, I would sit in there with her and she would have fun jumping around me."

One of Gem's favourite games was trying to nibble on Katherine's long brown ponytail. "Wombats love eating hair for some reason," she says with a laugh. "Gem gave it a nice trim with her powerful teeth." Gem also had a 'comfort toy' that was soft but also strong enough to stand up to wombat combat. "Biting is really important to wombats. It's one of the main ways they have to defend themselves. They practise when they're little by mouthing Mum but not putting any pressure on the bite. As the months go by, they use more and more pressure," explains Katherine.

A human mother would not react well to a bum bite.

But wombats have a bum shield: four bony plates fused together, covered in strong flexible cartilage; a layer of fat, thick skin; and finally, coarse fur. It's one of their main defences against dingoes and foxes. If a wombat is chased, it will dive partway into its burrow, blocking the entrance with its armoured bum. Most predators will give up after a few attempted bites. But if they don't, the armoured bum becomes a deadly battering ram. The wombat edges in just enough to allow the fox or dingo to get its head into the burrow entrance, then it uses that steel-hard butt to slam the predator's head against the roof or wall, crushing its skull.

With such good defences, wombat mothers don't mind their babies' bum bites very much, but it's a different story for zookeepers. Katherine says they used Gem's toy as a shield. "She learned to bite on the toy, not on us."

Those sharp, strong teeth proved their worth as Gem was gradually weaned from milk, now a youngster feeding on grasses, sedges and rushes. Some of those plants are very tough, but wombat teeth slice and grind them as if they were lettuce.

NEVER-ENDING TEETH

Humans have two sets of teeth: first 'baby' or 'milk' teeth, then 'adult' or 'meat' teeth. Generally, baby teeth start to appear between six and 12 months of age, and fall out one by one between the ages of six and 12. They are replaced by adult teeth, which are rooted to the jaw by a closed-off root canal. If you damage your adult teeth – for example, if one gets decayed and needs a filling – the damage is permanent. Wombat teeth are very different to ours, and to other marsupials', but very similar to rodent teeth. On their top jaw they have two incisors (front teeth) with a big gap before molars for grinding at the back – much like rats, squirrels and beavers. And like those rodents, the root canal does not close off, allowing wombats' teeth to grow continuously throughout their lives. This means that they can tear through the toughest native grasses year after year without their teeth ever wearing out.

By the time Gem was nine months old, her sleepovers with Katherine had come to an end; she had outgrown her transport pack.

But their bond remained. After wild joeys venture out of the pouch, they follow Mum's feet wherever they go. So Gem tracked Katherine's feet. "She'd walk so close behind, she'd clip my heels," recalls Katherine.

For Katherine, nothing puts a smile on the face faster than taking a walk with a baby wombat. As Gem grew older, she would start doing 'zoomies' – checking out the world, then dashing back to safety, back and forth like a furry pinball. Katherine's ambling baby wombat was turning into a speed demon!

Most people think that wombats just waddle along. But their short legs have tremendous launch power. Each foot is splayed wide, like a spade, giving it a large surface area to maximise power. "Most people have no idea these animals can outrun us," says Katherine. "Over a distance of 150 metres they can reach 40 kilometres per hour. The top six of the Men's 100-Metre Olympic finalists are the only people in the world who are faster than them."

When Gem tired of zoomies, it was time for a really

good scratch. "That hard plate goes from the hips all the way to the rear end. I'd scratch the edges of the plate around the hips and under the belly and Gem would roll over and act like she was in heaven," says Katherine.

As Gem passed her first birthday, it was time to get her accustomed to the main sanctuary enclosure. The animal hospital at Healesville has glass walls that enable visitors to see the recovering animals and even watch animal surgery and autopsies. But the noise there is muted. Gem was going to find the main sanctuary a lot louder. To help her adjust, Katherine brought other zoo staff into her room in the animal hospital. At first they just had a good old human chat in her presence. Then they started including the excited shouts and whoops that people make at zoos.

Soon Gem was ready for 'close-up encounters', where zoo visitors can spend a few minutes interacting with animals. The young wombat was fine around humans because she had been hand-reared and was still young. But Katherine knew Gem would outgrow this interactive role sooner rather than later. "You can have a kind of playful interaction with wombats until they reach what you might call their teenage years," she says.

Once they reach 15 to 18 months old, they tend to become aggressive – it's part of separating themselves from their mothers before they eventually go off to make their own way in the world. One of the signs that wombats are moving into adolescence is their changing behaviour when they are taken for walks.

"Just like human teenagers, when they reach that stage they listen to you less," says Katherine. "Normally with a little one, if they lag behind and you want to call them to quickly catch up, you just shuffle your feet to make a scraping or rustling sound in the dirt and they'll come running. But when they hit that 'teenage' stage, they won't respond. And when you go towards them, they'll do a testing kind of play where they sneak off while making sure you're looking, then come back, then sneak off again, over and over."

As she turned two, Gem was still playful and affectionate – and she still loved her 'teddy', even though it was now as flat as a pancake – but she had grown to 24 kilograms, about the weight of an eight-year-old child, too big for close-up encounters. "At that size, even if she pushed her head into your calf quite gently while you were walking, she would make your leg buckle. Having her in people's laps was getting to be too much. But she'd still follow me around if I came into the enclosure to pick up poo. And she'd still sometimes do zoomies or get excited by the old koala tree boughs we bring in to the wombats as enrichment objects, running through the leaves just for fun.

"She also still loved her scratches, which most wombats do right through adulthood. But she grew out of liking to be picked up and cuddled." The keepers knew to be very careful where they scratched her. One thing that's almost guaranteed to make a wombat aggressive is being touched on the head. "It really riles them up. We tell everyone who works with them, 'For your life's sake, do not touch the head!'"

Because she knew Gem so well, Katherine was able to tell when she was moving into full adulthood, where wombats sleep for most of the day and don't have much use for company. But even now, when she is awake, Gem is often still happy to see Katherine, especially when the keeper is shovelling dirt. "Wombats are such strong, fierce diggers they are known as 'the bulldozers of the bush'. If you see a wombat exhibit and it's all dug up and hilly and bumpy, that's great because they're demonstrating normal behaviour. You really know how good they are at earth-moving when it's time to move the sand or earth they've dug up – it's such hard work! Sometimes if I am digging in Gem's enclosure, she'll get right between my feet. The dirt goes all over her, but she just doesn't care, because that's what her mum would do."

But even when they have hand-raised an animal, wise keepers like Katherine never take their charges for granted. The head of the animal hospital, Gerry Ross, says, "People think wombats are fluffy and cuddly, but they're actually a big ball of muscle and bone. If they're afraid and aggressive, they can charge you. The bony plate over their buttocks area makes it so hard to even get hold of them if they don't want you to, and you can't just pick them up because, apart from being so heavy, they roll themselves into a ball or spin themselves around and they can try to bite you."

Katherine agrees wholeheartedly. As an adult wombat, Gem is a powerful animal. But the keeper will also always fondly remember her time looking after the young orphan.

WHAT CAN I DO TO HELP?

Choose paper wisely to save wombat homes: Wipe for Wildlife by asking your family, school and clubs to switch to recycled toilet paper. Reuse scrap paper where you can, and for printing choose either recycled paper or paper that has Forest Stewardship Council (FSC) approval so you know it is ecofriendly.

Encourage animal-aware driving: Let the adults in your family know that wombats are among the Australian animals likely to venture onto roads at night.

Control your dogs: Don't let dogs run loose in areas where wombats live. Larger breeds have been known to attack and kill them.

9

Chew, Sleep, Repeat – and Leap

Koalas

The family who spotted the ball of grey fluff on the side of the road knew he was in trouble as soon as they saw him. The tiny koala was too small to be away from his mother. She had most likely been hit by a car and they could see her baby had been injured too. They bundled up the joey carefully and rushed him to Victoria's Healesville Sanctuary, an hour's drive away.

The vets named the joey Noojee – after the town nearest to where he'd been found. He weighed just 1.4 kilograms and they guessed he was 10 months old, an age when a koala joey spends most of its time holding tightly to its mother's back and still relies on her milk.

Noojee was very cold and hadn't been fed in a long time. The vets inserted a drip into his vein to deliver pain relief and fluids, and gave him a teddy to cling to in place of his mother. He quickly settled and they were able to carefully check him all over for injuries.

Noojee had a burst eardrum and, very worryingly, a broken nose. The koala's nose isn't just cute; it's essential. Koalas are the only animal in the world that feeds entirely on toxic eucalyptus leaves. They need their noses to carefully select the leaves that they can tolerate. They also need to be able to chew *a lot*. Eucalyptus leaves are tough, so koalas have to do a lot of grinding with their molars. If Noojee's nose and jaw couldn't be fixed, he would not be able to survive.

Soon the little guy was well enough to be released from intensive care, but he still needed looking after round-the-clock. Like Gem, the wombat in Chapter 8, he spent his days at the animal hospital but every evening one of the nurses took him home so that he could be fed and checked on through the night.

Once Noojee's wounds had healed, it was time for the vets to decide whether he should return to the bush. The accident had permanently shifted the front of his upper jaw a bit to the right. The vets worried it might get worse over time, affecting his ability to chew. It was too risky to release him back into the wild so Healesville's Koala Forest became Noojee's home. And it's clear that Noojee has made the most of it.

KOALAS: FAST FACTS

They are:

Mammals: The mothers make milk for their babies.

Marsupials: The tiny babies go straight into their mother's pouch after birth and stay there until they are big enough to move around on their own.

Mainly nocturnal: They are most active at night.

Their scientific name is: *Phascolarctos cinereus*, which translates to 'pouched grey bear' (*phaso* means 'pouched', *arctos* means 'bear' and *cinereus* means 'ashy grey'). Despite the name, koalas are not bears at all. But they looked that way to European settlers and the name stuck. Some people still wrongly refer to them as 'koala bears'.

Their closest living relative is: the wombat.

Their babies are called: joeys.

Their average lifespan is: 10 to 12 years in the wild; up to 20 in captivity.

They are the only animal: that can survive solely on eucalyptus leaves. They do occasionally eat leaves from other trees, such as paperbark and bloodwood, but mainly stick to eucalypts. Two other mammals can safely eat the leaves, the greater glider and the ringtail possum, but unlike koalas, it makes up only a small part of their diet.

The biggest threats they face are: loss of habitat due to land-clearing for houses and roads; cars; and dogs.

Their conservation status is: Vulnerable for populations in Queensland, New South Wales and the ACT; Near Threatened for populations in Victoria.

Five years on, Noojee is a star attraction. He even has his own 'taxi service'.

In the afternoons, the visitors are treated to a koala feeding and a talk. "Often Noojee will come down to the ground while this is happening and he'll want to hop on whichever keeper is there," explains koala keeper Kristy Eriksen. "We'll pick him up and give him his cuddle, then he'll get a bit wriggly, which is an indication

ITCHY AND SCRATCHY AIR GUITAR

Most human-friendly koalas really enjoy getting a good scratch. They each have their own favourite spots, but males generally love to be scratched under the chin and along the chest, where they have a scent gland that they rub on trees to mark their territory. Just about every koala relishes a good scratch on the rump, where there is a thick pad that keeps them comfortable when they're wedged in the fork of a tree. It can be very funny watching a koala get a good old rump scratch from a favourite keeper like Kristy. In much the same way that when you rub a dog's back, its leg automatically starts going up and down in a scratching motion, a koala's front arm will start moving in response to the scratch. This looks, as Kristy says, just like it's playing air guitar.

that he wants to go to a tree. So we'll walk over and put him down and it's like he's going, 'Sweet, thanks.'"

After meeting Noojee and watching the way he lets the keepers hold him, some visitors assume that all koalas like a cuddle. This isn't so. As Kristy is always careful to point out, Noojee's enjoyment of human company is because he was hand-raised. Wild koalas prefer to keep to themselves high up in the trees.

Cuddly koala toys, koala onesies, koala keyrings, koala pencil cases – we see the animal's image so often and in so many places that it's easy to think we know all about it. But when it comes to real koalas, the fact that they mostly like alone-time instead of hugs is just one of the things that might surprise you. Another is that even though they eat the leaves of the eucalyptus (or gum) tree and there are billions of eucalyptus trees in Australia, they're one of the most expensive animals to feed in the zoo.

Australia may have close to 900 species of eucalypts but koalas will only eat the leaves of a few specific types. And their preferences can change with the seasons. Picky indeed.

So zoos that keep koalas need to maintain plantations of the correct species. It can take up to five years for the trees to grow large enough for their leaves to be harvested. For each koala, the zoo needs a staggering 1000 trees suitable for harvesting for food!

But even when the leaves are fresh and from exactly the right kind of trees, koalas won't eat just any leaf. The leaves of eucalypts are highly toxic to most animals. They contain chemicals that release the poison cyanide. Eucalypts produce these nasties to defend their leaves from being eaten. But 20 million years ago, the ancestors of modern koalas evolved a way to detoxify these poisons. This enabled them to survive high in the trees, entirely on a diet of eucalypt leaves, safe from predators below – like the marsupial lions that roamed Australia back then.

After scientists read the koala's DNA code (or genome) in 2018, they discovered the secret to the koala's detox superpower. Compared to other animals, koalas carry lots of extra genes for breaking down toxins. And their excellent sense of smell lets them detect which leaves are safe to eat and which contain more toxins than even they can cope with.

But while having their food source in the trees keeps them relatively safe from predators, it does not make for easy living. Eucalypt leaves are very low in nutritional value and they contain so much fibre that koalas' digestive systems have to work really hard just to break it down. It can take them up to five days to digest a meal.

In all of nature, koalas are the only other animal besides humans that have a unique set of fingerprints for every individual.

And that brings us to one of the biggest koala myths: that eating gum leaves makes them drugged or 'high'. Kristy shakes her head and laughs. "It's a line that I hear a lot, but it's not true at all." There are plenty of animals that survive by grazing on plants, such as sheep and giraffes. They are not sleepy in the same way koalas are because the plants they eat are much easier to digest and contain a lot more nutrients. Koalas sleep 18 to 20 hours a day, not because they're drugged, but because it's the way they have evolved in order to survive on the small amount of energy they get from their food.

Another myth is that koalas don't drink water. In fact, it's often wrongly claimed that their name comes from an Aboriginal word meaning 'no water' or 'no drink'. Mostly they get all the moisture they need from the leaves they eat, but in times of severe drought or if they have been stressed by an event such as a bushfire, they will seek out water. Perhaps you've seen one of the many touching photos of firefighters and wildlife carers holding out bottles of water as koalas drink from them.

Koalas can be fiercely aggressive when they feel threatened. Gerry Ross, a vet nurse for many years and now a manager at the Australian Wildlife Health Centre, says, "Koalas get stressed really easily. When they do, they can bite, and they've got arms and legs with big strong claws going everywhere, so trying to handle them safely can be quite difficult."

While koalas do sleep and rest a lot of the time, when they're awake they can be much more active than you might expect. Sprinting on all fours, they have been clocked at 30 kilometres per hour over short distances. They are also able to leap surprising distances from tree to tree, especially when they jump from a higher branch and land on a lower one. And they can get further than you'd think jumping up a trunk, either from a branch or from a standing start on the ground.

HOW TO KNOW IF KOALAS ARE AROUND

The colour of their fur and the fact that they are often motionless high up among the branches makes it hard to spot koalas unless you're very experienced. It's often much easier to tell if they're around from the signs they leave behind. If you're in a woodland that you think might be home to koalas, try looking down at the ground around the tree bases. The tell-tale sign you're seeking is koala poo: greenish-brown pellets about as long as the head of an adult's toothbrush and about as thick as a pencil. The more poo there is and the less dried out it looks, the more recently koalas have been there.

The next thing to look for is claw marks on the bark of the tree. Like us, koalas have five digits on their front paws, but they are arranged differently to our hands. Instead of four fingers and one thumb, they have three 'fingers' and two 'thumbs', giving them a really strong grip. When they climb, their sharp claws leave distinctive scratches in the bark.

Finally, you can listen out for them at night during the summer breeding season. The males are responsible for most of the noise, making a strange deep sound that would be very spooky if you heard it while you were camping and didn't know what it was. Called a 'bellow', it sounds like someone exaggeratedly pretending to snore while grunting at the same time and throwing a roar in at the end. The sound can travel up to a kilometre through the bush on a still night.

Some koalas use these skills to do a little exploring. Before she had a joey, Hazel, who lives with Noojee, sometimes liked to climb as high as she possibly could, occasionally to the surprise of visitors and keepers. But like other koalas Kristy has cared for, she never went too far.

“I’ve worked in three different zoos or sanctuaries and never had a case where a koala wandered and we weren’t able to find them. Nine times out of 10, they’ve simply climbed higher than they normally do. It’s usually pretty easy to look around and find them. But sometimes you don’t even have to look. I’ve known koalas that have decided to explore, gone seemingly out of sight and just settled in a tree until it was feeding time. Then they’ve climbed down and come back to be fed.”

If you're an animal lover, being a zookeeper might seem like the best job in the world. You feed them, train them and talk to the public about the cool things they do. Of course there's the less glamorous stuff too, like cleaning up their enclosures. And if you're a koala keeper there's an extra special duty of care: counting their poo. If the keeper suspects the koala is a bit off-colour, they will comb through their enclosure to gather and count poo pellets one by one – which could number 100 to 200 a day. Why? Changes in the way the poo looks or smells, or the amount of it, are the best ways to tell if they're unwell.

Koalas don't really show you if they're having a problem, says Kristy. "That makes being their keeper quite challenging because you need to get to know those individuals really, really well. You need to know exactly what's normal for each of them in order to pick up when something's not quite right." For instance, if a keeper sees a koala climbing lower down a tree than usual, that's enough of a concern to trigger a poo check. "It's not as gross as it might seem – because they only eat eucalyptus leaves it's probably the best-smelling poo around."

Koalas are considered 'Vulnerable' according to the IUCN Red List, which evaluates the extinction risk of species.

Like most of the animals in this book, the biggest threat to their survival is loss of habitat. Since the time of European settlement, 80 per cent of their eucalypt woodlands have been cleared for agriculture, cities and roads. Leaving patches of forest between houses and roads creates other problems. Like Noojee's mother, thousands of koalas die each year from being hit by cars as they try to cross roads, while others fall victim to pet dogs.

Then there's the increasing risk of bushfires. The 2009 Black Saturday fires, for example, burned 450,000 hectares of eastern Victoria, and killed 173 people and more than one million animals. With embers raining down, Healesville Sanctuary was at risk of being consumed by the firestorm. In an urgent operation the koalas living at the Sanctuary were evacuated to Melbourne Zoo, along with some of the other animals that were most at risk and that could be transported in such an emergency, including pregnant Tasmanian Devils, Helmeted Honeyeaters and dingoes. People who were able to help tried to keep the remaining animals safe by wetting everything down.

Over time, when the emergency was over and the area began to recover, the animals were gradually returned. But in the meantime, people started bringing injured animals into the Australian Wildlife Health Centre at Healesville Sanctuary. Some were burnt, some had suffered smoke inhalation, some had been orphaned.

Gerry's voice wavers as she recalls that time. She and the other staff worked round the clock to tend for the creatures that had been brought in. But even for those koalas that recovered, there was nothing left of the local forests for them to return to.

It took several months to find a new home for them. A smile breaks across Gerry's face as she recalls the day the koalas were finally released. "Watching them hop out of their transport boxes, then start climbing up the trees and calling out to the others. Oh, that was a good day."

WHAT CAN I DO TO HELP?

Use recycled paper: You mightn't be able to stop trees being cut down to build houses or roads, but you can do your bit to prevent them being logged for paper. Encourage your parents, your school and the other organisations you're involved with to choose recycled paper for everything from toilet rolls to your printer needs. When you're finished with a one-sided page, put it in a scrap-paper pile to use for drawing or scribbling notes.

Control your dog: If you have a dog and live in an area where there are koalas, it's very important not to let your pet run loose through the bush. If you live on land that has gum trees that are home to koalas, make sure your dog can't access that area at night, when koalas may be on the ground moving between the trees.

Take care on the roads: Encourage the adults in your family to watch out for wildlife when they are driving between dusk and dawn. If you see a koala (or another native animal) that's been hit, pull over safely and call your local wildlife rescue service for advice.

10

Fluffy but Fierce

Goodfellow's Tree-kangaroos

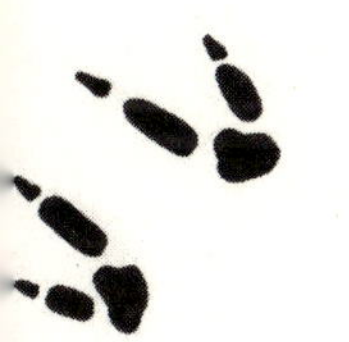

The first thing you notice about tree-kangaroos is their cute pointy faces and soft teddy-bear ears. They're much smaller than the kangaroos we're used to seeing, only about the size of a wallaby, and you might wish you could persuade one to come down from its branch so you could give it a cuddle. But zookeeper Katherine Sarris, who we first met in Chapter 8, knows that would be a terrible idea.

"If they attack, they will grab, bite and kick you all at the same time," she says. Her first lesson for new keepers in training is: "If you see them come down to the ground, exit the enclosure immediately."

It's not just humans who need to watch their back. Unlike more familiar members of the kangaroo family, these creatures are too aggressive to be housed with any other kind of other animal.

Yet the tree-kangaroos at Healesville Sanctuary have learned to trust Katherine. The female, Mani, will allow Katherine to open up her pouch and look inside – and even let her do it when a tiny newborn joey was growing in there. Such deep trust between an animal and a keeper doesn't happen by chance. It takes time and patience. And it requires a zookeeper to communicate on the animal's terms.

Mani is a Goodfellow's Tree-kangaroo. They live in the lush cool cloud forests on the eastern half of Papua New Guinea. But those forests are being lost to land clearing and palm oil plantations. The tree-kangaroo population has fallen by at least half over the past few decades. Because the area where they live is so rugged and remote, we don't know exactly how many are left. But we do know that they are in danger of extinction.

Zoos in Singapore, Germany and Australia have responded to the emergency with a plan to breed Goodfellow's Tree-kangaroos in captivity. To minimise inbreeding, mating pairs are drawn from different zoos after carefully examining their family trees. That's how Healesville Sanctuary acquired female Mani from the National Zoo & Aquarium in Canberra, and Bagam, a male from Krefeld Zoo in Germany.

Mani came first, arriving in 2016 when she was two.

TREE KANGAROOS: FAST FACTS

They are:

Mammals: The mothers make milk for their babies.

Marsupials: The tiny babies go straight into their mother's pouch after birth and stay there until they are big enough to move around on their own.

Neither nocturnal nor diurnal: They are active in short bursts throughout both day and night. In 1978, paleoanthropologist and lemur expert Ian Tattersall coined the term 'cathemeral' for such animals, originating from the Greek words for 'through' and 'the day'. While the word has yet to make it into mainstream dictionaries, it has been adopted by the International Union for the Conservation of Nature.

We have identified: 14 species so far, but evolutionary biologists believe it is highly likely that there are more still to be discovered.

Their babies are called: joeys.

Their lifespan is: uncertain in the wild; up to 23 years in captivity.

The biggest threats they face are: loss of habitat to mining, logging and palm oil plantations; and being hunted for food.

Their conservation status: ranges from Near Threatened for the Bennett's Tree-kangaroo and Lumholtz's Tree-kangaroo (the two found in Australia), to Critically Endangered for the Golden-Mantled and Wondiwoi Tree-kangaroos.

As soon as the young marsupial had settled into her tree-filled new home, the keepers began the slow process of training.

The first step was getting Mani used to their presence. Katherine and others on the team visited the enclosure briefly a few times a day to do clean-up and refresh the drinking water. Gradually they began to stay a little longer and offer avocado or pawpaw treats while carefully watching Mani's body language. "When they're really relaxed they go pigeon-toed," explains Katherine. "They hold onto the piece of food with both hands and just sit there comfortably, eating it."

PUTTING ANIMALS IN CONTROL

Zoos began more than 5000 years ago as amusements for kings and queens. These 'royal menageries' started to be opened to the public almost 300 years ago, but at first they were still for entertainment. There was often very little thought given to what the animals needed or how they might be feeling. Unfortunately, there are still zoos around the world where animals are kept in sub-standard conditions, but modern, forward-thinking zoos work completely differently, and Australia has some of the world's best.

Wildlife conservation expert Rachel Lowry says, "We have an incredible opportunity to help conserve these animals and their wild counterparts. One of the ways we do that is by addressing the threats in the wild, and breeding and releasing animals. That's a really important role zoos play now – there are species that would be extinct if it were not for zoos. The other is to help the community to love animals as much as we do, to educate people about the threats facing them and what we can all do to help.

"The role of a modern zoo is to provide a haven for animals. To provide exceptional care and ensure those animals are not just surviving, but thriving, that they've got a life worth living." The move to let animals drive their own care is a very big part of that, she says. "We want to try to provide animals with as much choice and control as possible because they know what they need better than we do. They know whether they're hot or cold, they know whether they want to get up high for a nice view, or whether they just want to go and sit over in the shade."

"But to give them that choice, you need to provide them with an elevated area and you need to provide them with shade – you need to provide them with so many different opportunities. We're getting better and better at doing that and I think if we fast-forward 50 years, we'll have taken it to a whole new level. I can see the day when our orang-utans are choosing their own climate controls within their exhibits and our animals will be able to flick a switch and move from one exhibit to another. We'll watch them walk above our heads over to an entirely new part of the zoo, because we'll have worked out ways to give them more and more choice all the time."

It turned out the key to Mani's heart was egg!

The pieces of boiled egg that Mani found irresistible allowed Katherine to take the most important step and examine Mani's pouch. "The belly area is a really personal area for any animal, and especially for a female," Katherine says.

It was really important to get to this point because even though Mani didn't yet have a mate, let alone a baby, everyone hoped she would become a mother. She needed to be very comfortable having her pouch examined before she got pregnant – it would be far too late to start then.

As with the pouches of other kangaroos, the interior is furless except for a narrow strip that acts like a runway. Once born the tiny babies crawl up their mother's furry belly, dive into the pouch and crawl along the furry runway to locate their mother's teats.

Tree-kangaroos have long, sharp, curved claws to climb vertical trunks and hang onto high branches. Those claws can do unintended damage during mating, making regular pouch checks very important: "The males can get a bit overzealous and they can really overstretch and scratch the pouch opening," says

Katherine. "If that happens and it's left untreated, it can lead to scar tissue, which can make it really difficult for the newborn to make it safely into the pouch."

Katherine didn't rush things. When she first opened the pouch, it was for just a few seconds at a time. This gradually got longer and longer, but only up to about 30 seconds, which is long enough for an experienced keeper to check on a joey. And the whole time, Katherine was watching out for any tightening of the muscles that control the pouch opening, indicating that Mani was getting stressed. If it ever began to happen, Katherine would stop immediately, always guided by what Mani was doing and how she was feeling.

Bagam arrived from Germany about a year later, and banana turned out to be his treat of choice. With the help of his tasty rewards, it didn't take Bagam too long to feel at home and build up his own bond with the keepers. "So then we could give him pats on the back. Not for the sake of touching him, but because it lets us feel the condition of his coat. We're feeling to make sure it's not too oily and not to dry – it's a sign of his health."

But Bagam didn't mind a good pat. In fact, he decided

he'd like a good scratch from the keepers, thank you very much. "He loves his chest scratches and his belly scratches and he actually likes to have them while he's eating," says Katherine. "Sometimes he really lies down into the scratch as he's eating."

Once Mani and Bagam had adjusted to life at Healesville, it was time to make an introduction. They may have been a good genetic match but that's no guarantee they'd be a 'love match'. In fact, there was the possibility they might seriously dislike each other. "They can become really aggressive, biting and harming each other, and possibly the keepers present as well," says Katherine.

When the sliding gate between their enclosures was opened, everyone was tense. With a sturdy garden rake to separate the animals and a hessian sack to throw over Bagam, Katherine's team were prepared for anything – attraction or aggression.

Bagam hopped through to meet Mani.

"She was perching up high and he saw her and started clicking his tongue, which meant he liked what he saw. Then he got closer, caught her scent and clearly liked that even more," says Katherine.

BLUE-EYED IN THE WILD

Unlike other tree-kangaroos, the Goodfellow's species have blue eyes. (The eye colour of Healesville Sanctuary's Mani is particularly special, according to experts, because it is such a bright shade.) But blue eyes are the exception among mammals. The blue-eyed spotted cuscus and Sclater's lemur are two other species that break the brown-eyed mould. Human eyes, of course, come in a huge range of colours – you can get brown, blue, green and grey within one family. But Spanish scientist Juan J. Negro, who has spent 25 years studying the subject, says this variability is limited to us and the animals we domesticated. Dogs, cats, horses, goats, camels and llamas can all have blue or brown eyes (or even yellow ones, in some cases), but other species, from deer to gorillas to elephants, only ever have one colour. There are exceptions – for instance, there are recorded cases of a koala and a coyote with blue eyes – but these are rare, one-off genetic mutations in brown-eyed species.

Mani wasn't quite ready to mate, but Bagam kept clicking and it was clear to the hugely relieved team that the pair were happy with each other.

The next question was whether Mani and Bagam would successfully produce a joey. Tree-kangaroos have the longest pregnancy of any marsupial – 45 days. So when mating did happen, the keepers counted forward on their calendars and circled the big day when a joey might make its appearance.

Pregnant marsupial mothers don't develop large bellies the way other mammals do, because their babies do most of their growth in the pouch. In the case of tree-kangaroos, the tiny hairless little pinkies they give birth to are only the size of a jellybean. If the baby makes it safely into the pouch, it clamps on to a teat, which swells up in its mouth and more or less secures the baby in place until it has grown large enough to poke its head out and take a look at the world. The joey stays in the pouch for nine to 10 months, until it's mature enough to pop out and explore the big wide world. Even after it 'moves out of home' and no longer sleeps in the pouch, it still returns for a drink to supplement the shrubs and fruits it has begun to eat.

The keepers kept watching the calendar but when the due date came they didn't observe a birth or any signs of one. Perhaps it had happened overnight. They could only hope everything had gone to plan. They forced themselves to wait 15 more days so as not to disturb the process. Then it was finally time to take a peek and answer the burning question: was there a baby in the pouch?

Katherine and two other keepers went in, boiled egg at the ready. One keeper gave Mani her reward and made sure she stayed calm and unstressed, while Katherine opened up the pouch. The other keeper pointed a camera over her shoulder to catch the moment on video.

"Sure enough, there was a joey attached to her teat," says Katherine. "It was very exciting! And Mani did very well, allowing us to enter that personal space. I was very careful to open the pouch just a little way so as not to overstretch it and I kept it open for no more than 30 seconds."

The baby was far too young for Katherine to tell what sex it was, but she checked its progress monthly, watching as the tail grew longer and the claws appeared

("Poor mumma!"). When the joey was couple of months old, Katherine saw that he was male. He was given the name Kofi, a New Guinea word for coffee, which was chosen not just because the zookeepers enjoy their lattes.

Coffee-growing may help save tree-kangaroos. It has already had a positive result for one of the Goodfellow's relatives, the Matschie's Tree-kangaroo. Tree-kangaroos live in misty cloud forests that cling to steep mountainsides. The moisture comes from condensation rather than rain, with drops forming on the moss- and lichen-covered trees, then dripping down onto the ferns and orchids below. With their extremely strong forearms, the tree-kangaroos rapidly shimmy up trees, and sit easily and securely 30 metres or more above the ground, letting their long tails hang down behind them. Unlike ground kangaroos and wallabies, they can move their back feet separately, and can walk backwards. They can also leap 12 metres or more from a tree to the ground – and several metres from one branch to another. But one thing they can't do is fight back against land-clearing.

Much of the land occupied by these rainforests

belongs to local people who are often very poor. So when companies offer them money to log their land or clear it to grow palm oil plantations, it's a hard offer to refuse. The Tree Kangaroo Conservation Program (TKCP) has come up with an alternative. It began as a conservation research project from Seattle's Woodland Park Zoo back in 1996. By building connections with local landowners and listening to their needs instead of telling them what to do, a plan was developed to find a way for the people of the area to make a living while still protecting their land. In 2009, the TKCP set up the country's first-ever conservation area, in the Huon Peninsula.

The protected land has now stretched out to cover a huge area, all of it controlled by locals who are supported by ecologists and animal specialists from around the world. Instead of clearing the land, as happens when palm-oil plantations are introduced, the local people now grow coffee beans. This can be done without devastating the landscape and the delicious coffee beans are in demand from other countries, so everyone wins – including the tree-kangaroos and other vulnerable forest species such as cassowaries and cuscus, whose home is protected and cared for.

The YUS conservation area, as it is known, now protects more than 760 square kms of land, encompassing 50 villages that are home to thousands of people. More than 600 farmers are already involved in the Coffee Conservation Project, allowing communities to afford education and health care. The plan is to keep growing.

Meanwhile, back in Australia, healthy, inquisitive young Kofi is a symbol of hope for his species. When he is between 15 and 18 months, he will be ready to separate from his parents. Just as Bagam travelled halfway across the world to become a father, Kofi could also find himself on an epic journey. Or it's possible he will stay in Australia. In addition to Healesville Sanctuary and Canberra's National Zoo & Aquarium, there are a number of other zoos here that are part of the Global Species Management Plan: Sydney's Taronga Zoo, the Perth and Adelaide Zoos, and Queensland's Currumbin Sanctuary. But then again, Kofi may travel as far as Singapore, Japan or the United Kingdom to become father to his own joeys.

In those countries and others around the world, thousands of people are working hard to save Kofi and his kind. These zookeepers, farmers, scientists and conservation educators have become warriors for wildlife, determined to use human ingenuity to find solutions to human-caused problems. Because no matter how fierce they can be when they want to, tree kangaroos – like so many other species – simply can't save themselves from extinction without our help.

WHAT CAN I DO TO HELP?

Join the campaign against unsustainable palm oil: When it is produced unsustainably, palm oil is the cause of the destruction of forests that are home to tree-kangaroos and many other species, including orang-utans, tigers and elephants. Palm oil is used in many different kinds of products, including food, cosmetics and toiletries. And we use an awful lot of it – it's in around half the food products on supermarket shelves, including lollies and chips. But it's often hidden under the bland description of 'vegetable oil'. That makes it very hard for people who care about animals to know which products to buy and which ones to avoid. Surveys have found that 95 per cent of Australians want to make it compulsory for products with palm oil to be clearly labelled – just as they have to be in Europe, the United States and Canada. That way, we can check what we're buying and make sure that if a product does contain palm oil it has the official Certified Sustainable Palm Oil (CSPO) seal of approval. If not, we can switch to a brand that does. But the rules haven't been changed yet. Search for #LabelPalmOilAlready to find out more.

ANYONE CAN HELP SAVE ANIMALS – JUST ASK LUKE

When Luke Eaton was eight he visited Melbourne Zoo one day, and what he saw there got him thinking.

He and his mum, Emily, had a lovely time looking at all the different animals and learning about their habitats and behaviours. Luke was most fascinated with the orang-utans, because they were real-life versions of his favourite soft toy, Tangy, who he'd had for as long as he could remember. Luke was captivated by the expression in the eyes of these great apes. They seemed so intelligent and curious. He got the feeling the orang-utans were watching the human visitors as much as the human visitors were watching them.

But moving around the exhibit, Luke read something that made him feel worried. Information boards explained that these magnificent animals are now Critically Endangered. One of the major reasons is that the jungles on the islands of Borneo and Sumatra, where the orang-utans live, are being torn down and replaced with plantations to produce palm oil.

Reading the information from the Zoo, Luke and Emily discovered that palm oil is in all kinds of products –

chips, lollies, noodles and shampoo. In fact, half of all the packaged items in supermarkets contain palm oil, even though they're often not labelled clearly. Even people who wanted to avoid palm oil found it hard to do so because you couldn't always tell whether it was in the product or not – or how much damage that palm oil had done to the environment. Zoos Victoria was trying todo something about this with its 'Don't Palm Us Off' campaign. Visitors to the Zoo were invited to sign a petition asking politicians to change the law so that companies had to clearly label any products containing palm oil and say whether it had been produced sustainably or not.

Luke was only little. It would have been easy for him to think he could never make a difference. But that didn't feel right. On the drive home he told his mum he wanted to do something, anything, to help the orang-utans. He decided to get a copy of the petition and try to collect some signatures himself.

It wasn't easy. He had to explain to people what he was doing and why it mattered over and over again. And when he tried setting up a table with his petition outside the stadium where he plays basketball, people crossed to the other side of the path to avoid him. They thought he was trying to sell them something. But Luke stuck with it, taking the petition everywhere he went, including school, after-school sport and weekend activities. As months passed he filled up one sheet of names after another.

Luke and his parents talked about what they might do with the petition. He asked if they could take it to Canberra to give it to the politicians who had the power to change the law. His mum and dad liked his enthusiasm, but they didn't think politicians would ever meet with them. They figured if they could drive up from Melbourne sometime in the school holidays maybe, just maybe, they could persuade the security guards at Parliament House to take the petition and pass it along.

But Zoos Victoria knew what an amazing job Luke was doing. They had arranged to take their original Zoo petition, which by now had 100,000 signatures, to Parliament House. The CEO of Zoos Victoria, Jenny Gray, was going to present it to a group of politicians who wanted to discuss the issue. When Luke reached 1000 signatures all on his own, Zoos Victoria were so impressed by what he'd achieved that they invited him and his parents to go to Canberra with Jenny.

It was an extremely exciting day, and although Luke felt very nervous when he had to speak to journalists and read a speech in front of TV cameras, he did a great job – having Tangy with him definitely helped. The politicians were so impressed they invited Luke and his parents and Jenny Gray to lunch at Parliament House. Afterwards, Zoos Victoria named Luke as one of their Conservation Heroes, another great honour.

Now 12, Luke continues to champion endangered animals, including Orange-bellied Parrots, Helmeted Honeyeaters, Leadbeater's Possums and Mountain Pygmy-possums. He's always coming up with new ideas and looking for opportunities to raise awareness.

One day, Luke was reading an article about the AFL and he saw a mention of animals in it. This gave Luke the idea to write to AFL player David Zaharakis to suggest that the AFL hold a conservation awareness day. He has also written to the prime minister and to the heads of big supermarket chains to share his concerns and ideas. His latest brainwave is a happy or sad orang-utan symbol that would flash up at the supermarket checkout, depending what was in the product you were buying.

Luke took part in a young people's brainstorming day on saving Endangered animals, and he even made a cake for the Threatened Species Day bake-off organised by Threatened Species Commissioner Dr Sally Box. His theme was Victoria's bird and animal emblems, both of which are featured in this book: the Helmeted Honeyeater and Leadbeater's Possum. His cake was impressive enough to win him a highly commended in the children's category!

In recognition of his continued commitment and all the work he has done to save animals, Zoos Victoria named him their Young Advocate of the Year for 2019 and gave him the huge honour of being part of the Zoos Victoria Hall of Fame.

Emily says Luke has taught her and his dad, Mark, a huge life lesson. "That first day when we were leaving the Zoo and Luke said he wanted to help, I'd never have thought that he could get this far. If someone says no to Luke he doesn't get discouraged, he just thinks about another path. He has taught us that there are no boundaries and no limits."

Luke says the reason he doesn't give up is because he loves animals and wants to help them, and it feels good knowing that he's done what he can. "I feel proud of myself and I think, *Wow, I've actually made a difference in something.*"

He adds that there are many ways to help. "Anyone can make a difference. You just have to try. If you're not comfortable standing up and speaking publicly that's okay (although by practising you'll get rid of your nerves). There are a lot of other ways. You can ask people to sign a petition or write a letter to a politician. You can talk to your parents about the things they buy at the shops and you can choose not to buy things that are hurting animals."

You can also get together with others who care, as Luke does. "Some friends and I started an Endangered Species Club at school. Each term we come up with a list of animals we're interested in and we research them. Then we vote to choose one and we work all term to help it. It doesn't matter who you are, there's something you can do."

Your donation details

☐ Please find enclosed a cheque for $______________
payable to Zoos Victoria

☐ Please Debit $____________ ☐ Visa ☐ Mastercard ☐ Amex

Card Number ☐☐☐☐-☐☐☐☐-☐☐☐☐-☐☐☐☐

Card Expiry Date _____ /_____

Name on Card ______________________________

Signature ______________________________

All donations over $2.00 are tax-deductible.

Please forward to:

Zoos Victoria
PO Box 74
Parkville 3052

Adopt an Animal

Zoos Victoria Animal Adopters are a group of passionate and generous people who are devoted to ensuring the many species in our care continue to thrive. Each month, they make an affordable donation that helps to fund our highest priority needs. Would you consider becoming an Animal Adopter?

Sign up online: donate.zoo.org.au/adoption

☐ Yes, I would like more information about becoming an Animal Adopter